Finding Comfort During Hard Times

Finding Comfort During Hard Times

A Guide to Healing after Disaster, Violence, and Other Community Trauma

Earl Johnson

ROWMAN & LITTLEFIELD
Lanham • Boulder • New York • London

Published by Rowman & Littlefield
An imprint of The Rowman & Littlefield Publishing Group, Inc.
4501 Forbes Boulevard, Suite 200, Lanham, Maryland 20706
www.rowman.com

6 Tinworth Street, London SE11 5AL

British Library Cataloguing in Publication Information Available

Library of Congress Cataloging-in-Publication Data

Name: Earl Johnson
Title: Finding Comfort During Hard Times: A Guide to Healing After Disaster, Violence, and
    Other Community Trauma
ISBN: 978-1-5381-2709-4 (cloth)
ISBN: 978-1-5381-1710-0 (electronic)

For Douglas

Contents

Acknowledgments

I would like to thank Kathy Green, Kristin Levine, Mike Roselli, and Matthew Mitola for reading this manuscript and helping shape it.

I would like to thank Suzanne Staszak-Silva for her extraordinary sensitivity as my editor and publisher and Elaine McGarraugh at Rowman and Littlefield.

I would like to thank Scott Widmeyer for his encouragement and support.

I would like to thank Jane Morgan, my mentor at national headquarters of the American Red Cross, the late Susan Hamilton and Marcia Kovach, and so many colleagues throughout the years there.

I would like to thank Tim Serban and the entire Red Cross spiritual care task force for their leadership, dedication, and sacrifices that have made spiritual care as a function of disaster response for the American Red Cross.

I would like to thank my family, particularly my husband, Douglas Ward, for his time and patience during this entire book process. I'd also like to thank Steve and Emily Ward and Andy Ward for your good advice at early stages of this manuscript. I would like to thank Paul Raushenbush, former religion editor of *The Huffington Post*.

I am profoundly grateful for my parents, Ruth Virginia Basye Johnson and Earl Edward Johnson, for their love and nurture, though they are deceased.

Introduction

On the morning of September 10, 2001, I walked in to my office, excited about starting a new job as a chaplain educator at Washington Hospital Center. My staff of fifteen chaplains was diverse, a Jesuit priest, a Pentecostal woman, a Methodist woman, an imam, an African American Adventist, and a Dominican brother. Little did I know that soon I would be swept up into a new career, working as a spiritual care specialist for disaster situations.

After the plane hit the Pentagon the next morning, Washington Hospital Center began discharging any patients they could, expecting hundreds of victims to be admitted. In the end, only fifteen people were brought in to the burn unit. The realization that there were no more patients, no more survivors, was devastating to all. It was my job as a hospital chaplain to provide spiritual and emotional comfort, not only for the victims, their families, and loved ones, but also for the doctors and nurses, the front office staff, and janitors. Everyone was struggling to comprehend the events of the day. What was there to say? How could I provide hope and solace to patients, colleagues, and friends?

The World Trade Center fell on my classroom on September 11, and eight years later I stood before 4,000 attendees at the National Disaster Medical System in Nashville and urged for the inclusion of disaster-trained professional chaplains to help the health and mental health capacity for mass fatality disasters as a national spokesman for the Red Cross. There were so many who had already brought such comfort to those impacted by disasters.

1

As devastating as this was, comforting those facing tragedy was not a new role for me. My passion for caring for others had started many years before at Yale Divinity School. Leaving New Haven, I worked with Margaret Mead in Africa. I saw the consequences of IRA violence in London and experienced the unrest in Jerusalem firsthand, when a bomb was found on the bus I was riding. Eventually, I decided I wanted to return home and took an associate minister job at a local college town church in Missouri.

Then in the early 1980s, my life changed. I came out as a gay man, moved to New York City, and started working in the fashion industry. This was the height of the AIDS epidemic and it hit that industry hard. After five years, with many of my friends and colleagues suffering from HIV and AIDS, I made the decision to give up my career in fashion and become a hospital chaplain. My specialty would be working with AIDS patients, many of whom I knew socially or professionally.

I returned to active ministry through hospital chaplaincy in 1994. I trained at New York-Cornell, Memorial Sloan Kettering Cancer Center, and New York Methodist Hospitals. I was hired by Cabrini Medical Center, in part, because I was a board-certified chaplain who also happened to be gay and "out." I could actively support patients who had been abused by religion and disowned by their families because they were gay and also had AIDS.

I loved Cabrini, now closed, because the hospital, with its core group of dedicated elderly Italian and other Catholic nuns, was one of the first to admit AIDS patients, even before the world knew what it was. This was a time of not touching door handles or using public water fountains. In those first years, thousands would die until protease inhibitors started to save so many infected with HIV. It was also a time of staff support groups for those who were dealing with the emotional impact of daily fatalities and "failure to thrive." It was not unusual to hear Donna Summer played at a memorial service. Oftentimes, the professional intersected with the personal. I would sometime walk into a room and realize the patient was someone I knew. I met my husband through a couple who were living with HIV/AIDS, who are alive today because of treatment advances and life-saving research. I remember the dead, perpetual grief, and a time when sex could mean death.

That experience taught me so much about how dealing with anticipated death allows us to appreciate our lives and spirit. Eventually, it led me to Washington, DC, on that fateful day in September.

As a board-certified chaplain, I have responded to mass fatality disasters across the country, including September 11, Hurricane Katrina, the Virginia Tech shooting, the Haiti earthquake, and the Orlando Pulse nightclub shooting. I have worked for the Red Cross as a spiritual care founder and have been featured as an expert in my field on CNN's *State of the Union* and on MSNBC.

Disasters do not discriminate between culture, race, class, or geography. This is not an issue affecting small pockets of unlucky people. The whole country has been touched by tragedy: Hurricane Sandy; the Boston Marathon bombing; the shootings at the churches and synagogues in North Carolina, Texas, and Pennsylvania; Sandy Hook Elementary School; Columbine; the Aurora movie theater. Since the beginning of this project, there has been the Paris and Las Vegas shooting; the hurricanes in Texas, Florida, and Puerto Rico; California wildfires and mudslides; the Parkland school shooting and the shooting in New Zealand. Through news and social media, it sometimes feels like we are exposed to one tragedy after another. The issue of how to respond to mass fatality disasters is, unfortunately, not going away.

In every place touched by disaster, people are longing for hope and comfort, striving to find purpose and meaning. After Hurricane Katrina alone there were 250,000 volunteers. People want to give and receive comfort from each other after these tragedies, but what exactly should they do? How should and could they respond? How do you talk to children about mass shootings or provide support to someone who has lost a loved one? How much can we endure?

Comfort answers these questions and many more. It is a book about easing grief and trauma after unimaginable horrors—plane crashes and mass murders, deadly tornadoes and terrorist acts. *Comfort* includes my personal recollections of responding to tragedy, combined with a practical application of what I have learned over the years. The book walks readers through the cycle of disaster care, using my firsthand experiences as examples. *Comfort* discusses the joys and stresses of volunteering (and managing volunteers) during and after disasters. It shows readers how their understanding of everyday trauma can help them respond to large-scale events. Finally, *Comfort* addresses the realities of dealing with special populations (children, elderly, etc.), as well as offering suggestions and guidance for the future.

Comfort provides the language of emotional and spiritual care and shares valuable wisdom gained from those who have worked in the worst of the worst situations. Whether you're a spiritual care professional, the victim of a disaster, a family member, or watching a disaster unfold on TV, *Comfort* gives the reader guidance and support, including actions and words to use. *Comfort* provides hope and strength to those dealing with a disaster, showing how posttraumatic growth is possible even after unspeakable trauma. It's not always easy, but it is possible.

I know this, because of my own personal and professional experiences. Let us go back to that day in September at Washington Hospital Center. As a hospital chaplain, you are trained to respond with care and compassion to people of all faiths (or no faith) even if their belief system is not the same as your own. When a request for a chaplain is made, whoever is on-call responds. And so when a family member of one of the burn victims from the Pentagon asked for spiritual support, the chaplain on-call was an imam from Saudi Arabia. The appearance of a Saudi Arab, a Muslim, responding to a victim of this terrorist attack caused a moment of initial shock. Would he be able to comfort this family?

When responding to someone in a traumatic situation, you have about ten seconds to get them to trust you, to figure out if you can help. If yes, wonderful—help. If not, get out of the way and find someone else for them to talk to. But either way, you can't take it personally. So in this moment, the imam introduced himself as the chaplain on-call and waited. After a moment—a pause, a heartbeat—the family accepted his help. They ended up praying together.

Comfort is all about providing this kind of support and care, bringing people together under the worst of circumstances and allowing them to find purpose, meaning, and hope.

Chapter One

Preparing for a Disaster

Where Comfort Begins

THE HISTORICAL PERSPECTIVE

When asked to speak about disaster preparedness, I always start my presentation by stating that Noah's Ark was the first disaster emergency response vehicle.

From Ebola in Liberia to locusts in ancient Egypt, from bridge collapses in Minneapolis to volcanic eruptions in Pompei, from the Asian tsunamis to the Spanish Flu epidemic of 1918, disasters are a major part of human and natural history, and not just natural disasters: Jonestown cult members drank the Kool-Aid in 1978; great fires burned Rome (AD 64), London (1666), and Chicago (1871); Jack the Ripper terrorized London in 1888; unfathomable and immense numbers of mass murders were committed during the Holocaust. From the Bhopal gas leak to the Buffalo Creek flood, the trauma inflicted by everyday and large-scale disasters is real and significant. No one is immune. Disasters strike rich and poor alike. Disasters inflict widespread physical damage and destruction, but also long-term psychological and spiritual wounds. The physical pain may heal, but the emotional and spiritual pain may never end without intervention and treatment. The damage is done both to the survivors and the responders.

As a child of the 1950s, I grew up in the age of "Duck and Cover," when fear of nuclear war was at its highest. My Uncle Dean and Aunt

Ruby built a fallout shelter on their farm in rural Missouri, using it to store canned beans and for tornado warnings, as well as a safeguard against a nuclear attack. My father was hired as a backup resource by the Air Force. They asked him to use one of his trucks from his towing business to pry off the cover of the Minuteman missile silo if it failed to open during a nuclear attack. I remember feeling both proud and horrified.

Today the scale and scope of disasters seems to have increased. Disasters once reported locally now cause worldwide stress and worry. One hundred years ago would anyone outside of Thailand have heard of the boys stuck in a cave? With the advent of technology, one cellphone connected to the internet can broadcast catastrophic news instantaneously around the world. Due to the expansion of all forms of media, I experienced, albeit from a distance, the assassinations of John F. Kennedy, Martin Luther King Jr., Robert F. Kennedy; the Challenger explosion; Midwest floods, hurricanes, tornadoes, and other killer weather; Waco, the Oklahoma federal building bombing, and Columbine. A bomb was found on a bus I was riding in Jerusalem. I ran by IRA bomb debris during the London Marathon in 1997. And then came the terrorism of September 11, 2001.

THE INDUSTRY OF DISASTER PREPAREDNESS

The September 11 attacks on our nation precipitated an explosion of disaster preparedness activities—preparedness and mitigation, rescue and recovery, mass fatality management, and all-hazard training. Faith-based disaster response organizations, which had traditionally taken the lead in disaster response and recovery, were simply too small and underfunded to meet these new needs of disaster preparedness and response. Billions in government funds were dedicated to homeland security, and an entire new industry of disaster preparedness sprang up. In the Bible, there's before the flood and after the flood; in the world of disaster preparedness in the United States, there's before and after that crystal clear late summer day.

With 9/11 came the realization that no one private organization or government agency had the human and material resources to meet all the immediate needs of those so profoundly impacted. There was room for everyone. Prayers are welcome, but food, water, and shelter are essential. Both provide comfort. Now, communities, towns, and cities create disaster plans and evacuation routes. Neighborhoods and even individual households are encouraged to do the same. Disaster preparedness was suddenly big business. Today there are disaster "kits" one can buy online and disaster preparedness trainings, from the government (Federal Emergency Management Agency [FEMA]) to private security corporations, for the threat of international and domestic terrorism.

The September 11 attacks were both horrible and traumatic. They were broadcast globally from the world's media and financial capital and seared into the consciousness of both the patriot and the idealist, the pacifist and the warrior. Using innocent civilians as hostages and commercial airliners as weapons brought the global war on terrorism into being and onto the nation's shores. Disaster was not someplace else in the world. Disaster was here.

As a result of the terrorist attack on our nation, almost every locality suddenly felt vulnerable. Doing something feels better than doing nothing, and after 9/11, the threat of domestic terrorism became real. Suddenly there was a need for widespread disaster education, with many anticipating another attack, and a nation stepped forward seeking to know what to do and how government would meet their needs to protect, serve, evacuate, shelter, and comfort.

One crucial fact emerged—those with basic disaster training had less compassion fatigue and burnout than those who simply tried to assist without a basic working knowledge of the unique aspects of responding to a disaster. This was based upon a study of 800 spiritual care professionals working after 9/11 in disaster service delivery sites and published in the *Journal of Nervous Diseases*. Red Cross offers Disaster 101 and FEMA offers disaster preparedness and response as an online course. Even a few hours of training made a difference in knowing what to anticipate, growing awareness, and understanding the unique aspects of disaster.[1]

EVERYONE NEEDS A DISASTER PLAN

One of the changes that came out of 9/11 was a new emphasis on disaster planning. From government facilities to home daycares, everyone is encouraged to come up with guidelines on what to do in case of the once unimaginable happening again.

Government disaster plans may include citywide or regional evacuations and, for first responders, active disaster drills. Who is in charge is not just left to chance or who shows up. Most government offices now use the Incident Command System (ICS), which was developed in the 1970s as a way to more effectively deal with wildfires in California. It was found that the main problem in responding to fires was not a lack of resources but inadequate management. ICS provides a framework for first responders, so that everyone understands the command structure and their role in the response efforts.

Businesses should have a disaster plan as well as a Continuity of Operations Plan (COOP) as a best practice. This should not be just an occasional fire drill but a fully itemized and orchestrated disaster plan. What would happen if the brick-and-mortar part of one's business is destroyed by a bomb or a hurricane? Could the business survive? Does the business have a backup computer system or access to the Cloud? What happens if your office is lost in a fire? These concerns, as well as many others, should be covered in a COOP, so that if something catastrophic happens, leadership and managers know what to do to minimize disruptions and maintain critical operations. Even with so much telecommuting and working from the road or home, having a COOP is reassuring and a comfort, knowing that one's livelihood won't evaporate even if one's workplace is destroyed.

Schools have moved beyond the fire drill and now have plans for many different types of threats. Schools in Oklahoma are building reinforced safe rooms in memory of those children and teachers who died when walls and roofs collapsed during killer tornadoes. Disaster plans are required by state accreditation commissions today. All fifty states have experienced school shootings. Commercial organizations such as the ALICE Training Institute (Alert, Lockdown, Inform, Counter, Evacuate) provide school districts with active shooter scenarios and training programs.

Churches do not have divine protection from disaster either. The Department of Homeland Security/Office of Faith-based and Neighborhood Preparedness consults regularly with congregations about active shooter prevention and mitigation and other basic disaster planning. Since many houses of worship are also used as community shelters, it is vital to have a disaster plan for feeding, sheltering, counseling, and other emergency services. Bulk foodstuffs and bedding are stockpiled in various locations around the country, however huge warehouses are not practical for the faith community and those are generally left up to government.

Families need disaster plans, too. Today adequate warning and alert systems exist that should give families opportunities to prepare and possibly evacuate, so it's good to have a bit more of a plan than simply going to a corner of the basement in the event of a hurricane or lying down in a bathtub during a tornado. At the very least, families should have a plan designating a meeting point in case communications are shut down, emergency contact numbers, and have enough supplies stockpiled in one's house for up to ninety-six hours (be sure to include food and water for the dog and cat). Have a disaster kit with batteries, flashlights, first aid, medicines, and other necessities.

For myself, I know that in the event of an emergency if I can't get to our condo, I will go to our cabin in the woods. If possible, I will then text relatives of our safety. We have supplies in the cabin to support ourselves for a week. It is a privilege having a second home, and others may choose to rendezvous at grandma's or Aunt Jenny and Uncle Tim's. At our cabin, we have large multigallon containers of water, a solar-powered radio, candles, flashlights with batteries, lots of macaroni and cheese and tuna fish, and a backup generator. We have bags of dog food in water-tight containers and a first-aid kit. Although we are isolated, we have extra inflatable beds for company. There is a well and firewood. I am comforted by my disaster plan.

Disasters bring out the best and worst in people, and they exacerbate preexisting conditions like illness, racism, and other forms of discrimination based upon difference. During a tornado in Alabama in 2011, a black family was not allowed in the basement shelter of a white church. One recent active shooter training failed to address the needs of a transgender student in Virginia, who was not allowed in either the boys or girls locker rooms when evacuated and barricaded to protect students. This is unacceptable. Having and practicing a disaster plan allows us a chance to become aware of and deal with these and any other forms of discrimination.

HARD AND SOFT TARGETS

Another aspect to consider when developing a disaster plan is whether the place you are trying to protect is a hard target or a soft target. Hard targets are places like military bases, police or fire stations, or armories—anywhere that is on constant alert. A soft target is a gathering at a theater, church, shopping center, or sporting event—anywhere that is not on constant alert. Emergency operations centers always open for large-scale soft targets like the Super Bowl, the Olympics, a Pope's visit, or a political party's national convention. Disaster preparedness plans include ramping up response operation leadership as well as staging supplies and resources including volunteers and management teams.

EVACUATIONS

Oftentimes, disaster preparedness plans may include a widespread evacuation plan. Whether the evacuation is triggered by a hurricane or earthquake, a chemical fire or a dirty bomb, you need to know what to do when it's time to get the hell out of Dodge.

Two million people tried to evacuate Houston for Hurricane Rita in 2005, but it was generally described as a failure due to traffic and insufficient resources. One group of senior citizens died when their evacuation bus caught fire outside of Dallas, a catastrophic loss of life.

The decision was made *not* to evacuate Houston for Hurricane Harvey in 2017 (due to the debacle of 2005), but then thousands had to be rescued from floodwaters in neighborhoods throughout the city and eighty-two people died. What constitutes an acceptable loss? Eighty-two lives? Two million on the road running out of food and gas? It becomes a difficult and sometimes political calculation.

Evacuations are supposed to be for everyone, with the assumption of transportation and privilege. But in New Orleans during Hurricane Katrina, not everyone had transportation or a place to go. Some residents chose not to evacuate for Hurricane Florence because they couldn't afford to pay the cost of gas and hotels, opting to ride it out at home instead.

SHELTER IN PLACE

In 2014, the hunt for the Boston Marathon bombers precipitated, for the first time in recent American history, a citywide command to shelter in place. This means staying where you are whether at work, home, or school. All disaster plans have a philosophical underpinning of public safety. When it is not possible or extremely dangerous to the public to evacuate, shelter in place is the next best option. Schools have these plans as well for active shooters and other emergencies. Current recommendations urge preparations for staying where you are for at least three days after an event—at your school, at your office, at home, at the airport, or at the mall. Staying at home, and out of the way of rescue/recovery efforts, can protect both the general public and first responders.

From the fallout shelters of the 1950s and 1960s, which some families built in their basements or backyards, to the large public shelters that were stocked with provisions for sheltering large groups in urban settings, all levels of government urge preparedness for natural and human-caused disasters. Sometimes, a school or other building needs to be quickly converted in an emergency to a shelter-in-place location. And as in any shelter, public health issues remain and are often heightened by the damage to local infrastructure. Can there be a flu outbreak in a shelter? Absolutely. Can shelters be quarantined? Yes. Should all shelter residents have background checks? Not immediately due to the disaster emergency. Shelter residents need to be mindful of their children and watchful. What can happen in society can happen in a shelter.

SOCIAL MEDIA ALERTS

In October 2018, FEMA sent out a message to everyone with a cellphone. Many felt it was valuable; some felt it was a nuisance. AMBER alerts are common now. I receive flash flood warnings and power outage reports over my cellphone regardless of the hour. It's the business model that has been adopted to alert customers, families, and individuals. Many children have their own personal cellphones and can communicate directly with their parents or caregivers. If evacuated or hospitalized, many simply text their parents where they are and where they are being taken. Just several years before, parents had to be sent to a central location to meet and collect their children.

How to use media alerts most effectively is an evolving issue. But for an alert system to be meaningful, worthwhile, and effective, you still have to get people to know about and sign up for them.

GETTING PEOPLE TO PREPARE
(BUT IT WON'T HAPPEN TO ME!)

There's only one problem with all these disaster plans: studies published recently in *The New York Times* show that fully one-third of the population is averse to disaster preparedness! There are a number of reasons for their hesitation. For some, disaster preparedness feels like a self-fulfilling prophecy. If you plan for a disaster, their thinking goes, a disaster is more likely to happen. Other have the belief that in a disaster, the Lord will provide, that human beings do not really have to do anything, that some benevolent Creator will swoop in the last minute and rescue or save believers. This belief system can often be countered with the comeback, "Jesus is not going to be driving the rescue boat!"

However, there is also the reality that many Americans live paycheck to paycheck, and the ideal of stockpiling food for emergencies just isn't a financial option. There are others with full pantries that are destroyed in disasters. The most essential needs in a disaster are information and reassurance. Information can be about evacuations and shelters, but primarily have to do with the safety and welfare of family members and pets. What one does to prepare for disaster, can comfort when a disaster happens. If the communications grid isn't destroyed, I can let you know with my cellphone that I am okay. I am safe and well. That will be the ultimate comfort.

Ultimately, the purpose of all these disaster plans and preparations is to lessen the chances of loss of life. Knowing what role one is playing in the disaster response structure is essential. You are part of a team. You don't have to do everything. Simply having a plan can decrease anxiety.

But having a plan is not enough—you need to practice carrying it out.

EMERGENCY DRILLS

Emergency drills serve multiple purposes. Schools have fire drills so student will know where to go in an emergency, reducing confusion. However, drills can also expose flaws in a disaster plan, such as an escape route that is blocked by a locked door.

And drills aren't only for children. Hospitals and first responders routinely practice disaster response. When I was at Cabrini Hospital in lower Manhattan, we conducted a drill one day, preparing for a dirty bomb. One of the nuns helping with the exercise ran into the lobby to help receive victims. She was promptly told by exercise organizers that she had "died," because in responding to a dirty bomb, dangerous materials are more concentrated on lower levels. The proper response would have been to evacuate patients to higher floors. Chagrined, she sat out the rest of the exercise, but she will certainly never forget what to do if such a disaster ever occurs.

Teachers may undergo active shooter training with the trainers wielding nerf guns. This is not preparedness theater. This is standard operating procedure and a best practice for educators and students today. Drills can highlight evolving best practices as well. The newest recommendation in school shootings is to evacuate earlier instead of waiting for help to arrive. A gun can blow open a locked classroom door, a barricaded door offers more protections longer, but an empty classroom is the ultimate protection. Having patience for the police or a SWAT team to arrive is no longer considered a best practice. Disaster plans evolve and adapt to changing situations, reality, and research.

My own neighborhood SWAT team recently conducted a drill involving dozens of plainclothes officers immediately materializing out of nowhere for a practice scenario that involved rescuing hostages. Do these simulations make me feel safer? Yes. Thankfully we received a community notice in advance that this was just a drill.

After action reports on September 11 faulted the government for not being imaginative enough in scale and scope for potential disasters, the federal government started to create and rehearse many catastrophic disaster scenarios. While at the Red Cross, I participated in catastrophic mass casualty drills with the U.S. military North American Command (NORTHCOM) in Colorado Springs. These drills included imagined events such as multiple hijacked airliners, a mass fatality plane crash, and an earthquake "killing" thousands along the New Madrid fault.

Another scenario featured a dirty bomb exploding in Washington, DC, but I stopped playing that disaster preparedness "game" immediately since I (and my family, colleagues, and friends) would have been killed if such an event occurred. I did not share the glee in the room for such an exercise. There are disaster "junkies" who get an adrenalin rush when disasters are predicted and occur. In Haiti, it was a red flag for disaster managers when a colleague would get excited every time another body was found. He was reassigned away from that disaster arena.

For some, disasters and drills are entertainment—diversions from lengthy, dry lectures. But for others, living close to hard targets and harm's way, they can be painful, emotional reminders that threats are real and proximity to potential targets carry immense burdens. While no one wants to live in fear, part of disaster preparedness is realizing disasters are not just things on television that happen to other people who live far away. Disasters can occur anywhere to people like you and me. They don't discriminate between rich and poor or care about your age or race, but with just a little advance work, we can all feel a little more prepared.

THE COMFORT OF KNOWING WHERE YOUR KIDS ARE

An essential part of disaster preparation including the emotional and spiritual part are the concrete plans for your family. There are various sources for preparations but they all share one thing in common: making a plan for the next emergency.

Can one imagine what might occur, as has in the past, for a complete shutdown of the power grid and its impact on our connectedness? It's not just the millennials who will be most impacted, but all of us. On September 11, circuits were overloaded and cellphones and Blackberries were rendered useless. During the New York blackout (any of them), again, basic communication wasn't possible. Chaplains had walkie-talkies that worked on batteries and satellite signals to deploy emotional and spiritual care comforters to those who were forced to walk home to the Bronx, Brooklyn, and Queens en masse. Keeping calm and offering consolation was invaluable during the immense power shutdown.

But until you know where your family is—your spouse, children, parents, and close friends—you really will not be able to comfort anybody. You will be incredibly distracted and unable to listen to those needing to be comforted and reassured. Disasters are inconvenient and chaotic, and everyone may not be home when they occur. Children may be at school, and parents may be at work. Some will affect communication, and some will affect transportation, or both. Disasters will have an impact on young and old, but they will express their need for comfort in very different ways. One may face elements of mobility and medication, others may simply shut down in anger and rage because their smartphones are rendered deaf and dumb.

So, make a plan with the following four components:

1. Start with a family meeting to discuss what might occur in an emergency. What is our plan?
2. What does the family need? Be specific.
3. Write it down.
4. Practice it.

First of all, during the family meeting discuss and determine how one will receive news of an emergency and warnings. Is there a battery-powered radio in the household? (Alexa may be unable to speak to you.) Are there shelters in the house like basement game rooms or man caves? I live in Washington, DC, and evacuation routes are a big deal. Where do I go if I must evacuate my home? And make sure school and work have evacuation plans too that the whole family knows about. Finally, how will we talk or find each other if we are separated?

Knowing where the family has a predetermined meeting place if an emergency occurs will be extremely reassuring and comforting. By helping yourself, you will be in a position to help others and be of comfort. It may not be as simple as "go to grandma's house" or "go to the church or synagogue," but it starts one thinking about possibilities during extreme events like disaster emergencies.

Secondly, who am I responsible for? A real thought-provoking conversation starter that helps assess specific needs in a family. The baby, the great aunt, the elderly neighbor who lives alone, the student who is home from college, the pregnant daughter; basic household demographics must all be considered in making a plan. Each of them will have different needs—from dietary to medical needs (are they on oxygen, etc.?), different languages, cultural considerations, religious issues—all need to be considered in an emergency plan. After all, how can one comfort if basic needs are wanting or not being met. Other considerations may include locations frequented. Where does one go before or after work? Do they go to the gym or country club, to the soup kitchen? What about school-aged children? Are there after-school programs? And, finally, what about the pets. Some hurricane evacuees have left their dogs chained in the backyard during a rising flood, which is a very poor decision made in the heat of a family evacuation that was not well thought out. Pet rescues almost take as much time as human rescues in some disasters.

The third part after identifying all the possibilities and needs is to actually fill out and complete your family's disaster emergency plan. Realizing that text messages may get through where phone calls don't, make sure you include all forms of social media that may assist you in getting in touch with your family. Children and adults are becoming far more creative in communication methods, and it is good to have back-up if the phones don't work. Also important is medical and other information that may be helpful if one isn't capable of communicating to helpers and others.

Churches and businesses have disaster plans, and schools have disaster and lockdown plans, but it's important for families to have disaster plans, too. It is extremely reassuring and comforting to know the schools, communities, and hospitals regularly practice disaster scenarios from weather events to human-caused events like terrorism. Having an emergency plan for picking up children from school is comforting and basic. Not having a disaster plan today is unforgivable for those institutions that are caring for special needs populations like children and the elderly. Knowing what the plan entails and who to contact in an emergency is also basic. Will there be an emergency hotline set up just to handle calls from anxious parents? Will there be emergency meeting places for those impacted to go and await further instructions that are safe and convenient?

Will there be an out-of-town contact in case the destruction and devastation renders all communication out of commission? Does the family have an emergency meeting place outside the impacted area?

My family may try to reach a cabin in the mountains if the urban infrastructure is damaged or destroyed. Knowing that the family will rendezvous at grandma's house is a comfort, but there are many new families that may not have a grandma or distant contact.

Finally, don't expect all family members to remember what was discussed and decided. Practice the plan. For smaller children, one can make it a type of game or exhibition. There was actually guidance issued stating to think of a mass evacuation as an opportunity for your children to make new friends.

Try to communicate with various social media and smartphones. If you don't have a landline for your telephone (an increasing possibility), make sure you have extra batteries and chargers for sites you might use.

In summary, not only should one make a plan, they should also build a kit for emergencies (see chapter 6). That plan includes discussing and putting together an emergency disaster plan (think about what specific needs there will be for your family). Put the plan down on paper and circulate it to every member of the family, and, finally, take time to rehearse the plan. Know that there is a happy medium between Old Testament prophecy like "the sky is falling" and "scaring the heck out of everybody" with plans for an immediate Big One. [2]

There will be major differences between a comfort care plan for an urban area that is densely populated and a rural community where people live far away from one another. There are those who have historically had disaster plans in case of tornadoes or established hurricane evacuation routes. In simpler times, people may have gathered in the church basement or school gymnasium and shared casseroles and potluck if there was an emergency. Many privileged people have summer or vacation homes that they can evacuate to in a major emergency.

But emergency managers in the government working with the private sector need to be mindful of the privilege of evacuation, which may not be possible for the elderly and the poor. Having an emergency plan is not a luxury but a necessity today with threats of more intense weather, as well as fears of domestic and other terrorism. How can I comfort you if I don't know where to go and what to do? If I can't tell you reliable, basic emergency information, how can I comfort you?

WAYS TO COMFORT—PREPARING FOR A DISASTER

1. Take disaster training; even a basic course makes a difference. Knowing what to do may be a comfort when you are overwhelmed. Start with www.ready.gov or your local Red Cross.
2. Take a deep breath and make a plan. Write it down and post it. Once again, knowledge lessens anxiety.
3. Evaluate your basic needs and resources and build a disaster kit.
4. Talk to family, friends, colleagues, children—make sure they know what to do.
5. Don't let the stress of getting things "perfect" prevent you from doing anything at all.
6. Be flexible. Be confident in hospitality. Add another plate. Welcome those in need.
7. Designate a family member or friend to contact in an emergency and a meeting location.
8. Be patient. Have age-appropriate conversations with children and reassure them.

9. Be kind. Reassure the elderly and groups with special needs. Let a family define who is a member of their family including pets.
10. Be authentic. Personify hope and reason. Say what you mean and only what you know to be true. Do not pass along rumors. Be the nonanxious presence in the room.

NOTES

1. https://www.redcross.org/take-a-class/disaster-training
2. ready.gov

Chapter Two

The First Day

YOU REMEMBER WHERE YOU WERE

When Paris-bound TWA flight 800 went down in 1996 off Fire Island, New York, I was at Methodist Hospital in Brooklyn, working on my chaplain residency in the intensive care unit. When the space shuttle Columbia disintegrated upon reentry in 2003, I drove into the Disaster Operations Center at the Red Cross, wondering how to respond if part of the spaceship hit a bus or shopping center. For baby boomers, we can tell you where we were and what we were doing when President Kennedy was shot—I was cleaning basketballs as a team manager in junior high school. The same with the greatest generation: they can tell you where they were when Pearl Harbor was attacked, beginning American involvement in World War II. Most of the readers of this book probably have their own vivid memories of what they were doing on September 11, 2001.

When a tragedy occurs, you remember where you were and what you were doing.

As I write this, I've just found out a friend has died, found in his bathtub, and waves of emotion accompany me. I call his friend who is grateful but in shock. Death is a normal part of life, but when it comes unexpectedly, it can be hard to accept. Maybe it's not true, we think. Let me send a text message and see if he answers? Friends and family reach out and seek to comfort one another, but sometimes the void is too large, the silence is too vacant. To deny the reality is also normal. The pain otherwise would be too much.

This chapter will discuss what to do, how to provide comfort in those first few moments, when gut-wrenching pain and overwhelming sorrow has touched someone close to you.

WHAT TO EXPECT THE FIRST DAY

When we imagine learning bad news, we often envision a phone call— the police calling late at night about a car accident, a doctor calling with a cancer diagnosis. But news of a severe trauma is best told in person. When the military has to notify a family about their loved one's death, they send a duty officer (and often a chaplain) to the home. They do not phone ahead. The nonverbal message of an unannounced officer coming to the front door says it all.

If death occurs at a hospital, again, the family is not told over the phone. Instead, they are asked to come to the hospital, where they will be escorted into a private room, often adjacent to the emergency room. There will most likely be a couch or chairs, a table, and a box of tissues. There the physician (or sometimes a head nurse) will tell them about the death and ask if they have any questions. Hopefully, there is also a chaplain or other support person available to provide support after the medical professional must return to treating patients. Ideally, everyone should be told about a tragedy in a controlled and private situation by a trained professional.

However, it does not always work that way. Sometimes, one may directly witness an event. In 2006, some family and friends were still at the Lexington, Kentucky, airport when Comair flight 5191 tried to take off using the wrong runway and crashed and burned. On September 11, some people called their families from the hijacked planes to say good-bye. Teenagers at a Las Vegas country music concert in 2017 called their parents while the shooting was still going on. Today, with wide-spread news media, many of us learn about tragic events from even less-personal sources than a phone call: TV, social media, or even notifications on our phones. This instant communication can be reassuring, but it can also be traumatizing. The 2018 ballistic missile alert in Hawaii lasted thirty-eight minutes before a retraction could be sent out that it was a false alarm.

And what does it mean if you are unable to reach a loved one? Are the cell towers overloaded? Are they hiding in a closet, not answering their phone because they don't want to attract the attention of an active shooter? Or has something worse happened? After the Madrid train bombing in 2004, first responders spoke of hearing cellphones ringing in the rail cars where the dead lay. They knew these calls were from wives and mothers, husbands and fathers, and children who would never hear the voice of their loved one again. At some point, those calling might have guessed the truth too. But the cellphones kept ringing, hope against hope.

After learning about a tragedy, meeting places for family and friends spring up. The first is often the emergency room, where loved ones gather to await news on their loved one's condition. But an emergency room is limited in size and the number of grieving family members it can accommodate. Eventually, families are sent to another location where a reunification and notification center is established. In the Orlando nightclub shooting, this was at the Hampton Inn, which was adjacent to the hospital. In the case of an airline crash, airlines typically set up their reunification and notification center in an airport hotel. In the 2018 school shooting in Parkland, Florida, an elementary school down the block was used as a meeting place.

At the reunification and notification center, family members receive news and updates on the welfare of those being treated or, sometimes, notice of their loved one's death. This is where people are sent if they call the 1-800 number. Often, an "all hands on-deck" call is sent out for experienced counselors and companions to come to the reunification and notification center to help out.

GASPING FOR AIR:
PROVIDING COMFORT DURING THE FIRST DAY

It may be in a hospital waiting room or a police station, at an airport hotel, or even in your own living room—but how do you help someone who has just learned that their loved one has died in a plane crash or a mass shooting or other traumatic event? In order to comfort, we must think about the survivor's immediate needs.

First, be the nonanxious presence in the room and keep your focus on the person you're trying to comfort. Chaos and noise is a part of the notification process; throwing oneself on the ground, screaming, wailing, cursing, gasping for air, breaking something, or punching walls are not uncommon behaviors when someone learns that their loved one has passed away. Be prepared for and accepting of such responses. Part of spiritual care at this time is simply helping people breathe.

It's important to remember that family members receiving unanticipated death notifications may not be rational. Expect anything. State your name, who you are, and what you're doing there in the room with them. For example, "My name is Earl, and I'm a chaplain. I'm here to be with you." Then, stop talking. Don't be afraid of the silence. Don't fill up the space with words by saying whatever your own anxiety inspires you to say.

If they want to talk, listen to the person you're seeking to help. What are they asking for? Is it reasonable? Don't make promises you can't keep and only give out factual information. Remember, there is much being communicated that may be nonverbal—weeping, rocking, sobbing uncontrollably.

Comfort is about patience and flexibility, particularly as it relates to supporting family members of school shootings. All moms and dads want to know, "Where is my child?" That is vital, life-giving information, and until those questions are answered, be prepared to expect anything. Terror, as well as grief, is not rational or predictable. It can stimulate and provoke any behavior from breaking police lines to masquerading as a coroner.

At some point, you may want to ask, "Is there anyone you need to call?" This may include other family members, friends, faith community leaders, and so forth. After a tragedy, being able to get in touch with loved ones is as important as providing food and water. In recent disasters, people have used Facebook to check in and mark themselves safe or to search for loved ones. When cell towers were down after Hurricane Maria in Puerto Rico, apps such as WhatsApp provided a much-needed link to the outside world.

Generally, you're helping comfort someone in a private setting, but, if not, try for privacy. Large groups are very difficult to comfort, but one has a better chance at being supportive to an individual. You don't have to comfort everyone.

Do a quick assessment of the site where comfort is being offered. Are there weapons or anything that could possibly cause self-harm? Ask security to remove anything deemed potentially unsafe. Does your client need medication? Are they diabetic? Did they remember their glasses? After a nursing home fire in Arkansas, 150 residents were evacuated. The Red Cross had to coordinate with the local pharmacies to make sure the residents got the medicines they needed.

Be careful in offering prayer. If you've been able to start a conversation with someone, don't stop the conversation with prayer because of your own anxiety. If prayer is requested, ask what one would like prayers for—and be prepared for whatever the family member says. Their answer may be something totally unpredictable. For example, if someone was dealing with a domestic abuse situation before the tragedy, it's possible they may say something like, "Thanks for killing that son of a bitch." Don't judge, just listen.

Shortly after the crash of TWA flight 800, I received a call from a personal friend who had lost a family member in the crash. About forty members of the extended family had gathered at his apartment. However, they were surrounded by media and could not leave. He said they were looking for support, so I walked over to the apartment and introduced myself to his family.

How does one convey their condolences in such a high-profile death? First of all, by showing up. Their husband/brother/cousin had been lost and the body had not yet been recovered. Some started using gallows humor to cope: "He was flying first class, so we should get the body bag first." This is common after a horrific event, and I was not surprised by their comments. I saw my main role as simply being a calm presence they could lean on.

Indeed, it's usually helpful to reach out to a grieving family, unless you are specifically told not to. If you make a visit in person, there may be a gatekeeper, either real or self-proclaimed, who is answering the door. One will get a "feel" for the visit fairly quickly. If a visit seems too intrusive, a phone call or card may be more appropriate. The focus should stay on those who have lost the most and not you. One doesn't want to add to the chaos or make a scene. Being there and knowing when to leave are key components of comforting.

Finally, know that it's okay to make a referral when you know you're in over your head. There should always be a physician or health services on-call. Does someone need a sleeping pill or Valium? It is not all that unusual for someone to be hospitalized due to their overwhelming grief and reaction to a sudden, traumatic event. Don't worry, that's not your call. Use common sense, and if you ever find yourself in this situation, stay with the person until relief comes. Don't promise to do something you may not be able to do. Keep the focus on the present moment. Tomorrow, one can start planning the funeral or reading the will.

NEEDS OF FIRST RESPONDERS

It is important to remember that first responders may also be traumatized by what they witness. There may be spontaneous unaffiliated volunteers (SUVs) that pitch in and may be first on the scene and provide invaluable services. I'm reminded of the I-35 bridge collapse in Minneapolis where SUVs helped evacuate a school bus seconds after the event. However, even combat-trained physicians are not immune. Blood on the battlefield is expected; blood on the gymnasium floor is not.

The Pulse nightclub shooting in Orlando was carried out with military-grade weapons. One physician wore his blood-stained sneakers for days afterward in silent memory of those he treated and was unable to save. In a plane crash, the gate agent, janitor, or baggage clerk may need comfort or someone just to listen to them. Airline personnel often remember the faces of the young and old passengers, families and businessmen flying out on what they thought would be a routine trip.

When I worked at the Red Cross Disaster Operations Center, I became aware that my colleagues were dehydrating at their desks. So I had my husband bring in cases of water and operated a candy striper–style trolley, passing out the bottles in the office. During Katrina, my banter included, "It's a marathon, not a sprint," as I wore my marathon medals to add authenticity to my efforts to care for those who were taking care of so many. Sometimes, even a drink of water can provide comfort.

During the 2002 SARS outbreak in Canada, the management at one Toronto hospital made the decision to dismiss all nonessential personnel from the acute care campus; doctors and nurses would shelter in place for the treatment and care of their critically ill patients. Chaplains were among those excluded from the critical care core group. What followed was a spike in anxiety for both health care workers and patients. There was no one inside the bubble to deal with the profound emotional and spiritual issues identified in those early hours. There was no one to comfort.

The hospital management quickly realized the board-certified chaplains were, in fact, "essential" personnel. They were invited back to comfort the patients, doctors, and nurses, supporting them during a time of extreme stress and anxiety.

COMPLICATING FACTORS

Sometimes, there is a danger to the larger community that must be communicated, such as when an active shooter has not been apprehended. During the Virginia Tech shooting in 2007, in which a mentally ill student killed thirty-two fellow students and faculty members, some thought lives might have been saved if there had been a better way of notifying students and staff about what was going on. During a 2017 shooting in Tehama County, California, a school secretary called for an immediate lockdown, closing the school completely with the students inside. Her actions were credited with saving many teachers and students' lives.

Unfortunately, sometimes it isn't always clear who to contact after a tragedy. During the 2017 northern California wildfires, a helicopter carrying firefighters went down, killing everyone onboard. There was no passenger manifest because fighting roaring forest fires was treated almost like combat, and as soon as one helicopter took off, another one landed to be loaded. In that case, it was not possible to notify family members for days. Absences had to be checked first to make sure the nine firefighters who died had been accurately identified.

If you are in the awkward position of comforting someone who does not yet know their loved one's fate, remember the same ideas discussed earlier. They may be experiencing extreme anxiety. Try to turn off the television and limit their exposure. Only give information that you know to be true. Don't hug without permission. Don't hug if it makes you (or the other person) uncomfortable. Focus on now, not tomorrow's worries.

This anxiety can be especially intense when the victims include children. Until the child is reunited with his parents or caregiver, there are only small comforts—other family members and close friends that are there as advocates for the parents dealing with law enforcement and other public safety officials. You can stay with them and offer to make phone calls or monitor news outlets seeking updates, but I would help keep the media away unless the parents want to talk with the press in the hope that their child may hear them on television and know that they are somewhere close by.

Sometimes, especially if a tragedy is long or ongoing, you may need to end your support. You also have to sleep and eat. You may need to go take care of your own family. You may need to limit your exposure so that you do not experience secondary trauma. If possible, stay with the person until additional help arrives, so that you can trade off. And remember that caring for yourself is also important.

Dealing with tragedy is, of course, nothing new. My mother responded to a plane crash in 1929 when she was twelve years old. A TWA mail plane flying between Kansas City and St. Louis crashed near their farm. My mother flagged down the Greyhound bus so that the pilot could be taken to the hospital in Columbia. That was the rural equivalent of dialing 911.

These guidelines also apply to more private tragedies—a car accident, a suicide, or a cancer diagnosis. Sometimes, children can be traumatized by simply hearing about a tragic event that has happened to others. These same guidelines can be used to comfort them as well.

WAYS TO COMFORT—THE FIRST DAY

1. Start the conversation. Introduce yourself. Say your name and the group or community you are representing.
2. Be the nonanxious presence. Give emotional and spiritual comfort by just being there.
3. Listen. What is being requested? Only respond with factual information you know to be true. Don't make promises you can't keep.
4. Help make connections with loved ones. Ask, "May I call someone for you?" This may include family, friends, a faith community leader, or even a neighbor in case the family dog needs to be let out.
5. Is the area where you are offering comfort private? Is it safe? Understand how vulnerable mourners may be and report any predatory behavior to public safety officers.
6. Assess their needs. Do they need first aid? Do they need a coat or blanket? Is it raining and they could use an umbrella?
7. Offer reassurance and be sincere. Don't say, "Heaven needed another angel." There is no right thing to say, but so many wrong things. Remember, sometimes there are no words.

8. Keep the focus on the person you are trying to help and not "your" story. Respect personal space. Unless requested, do not assume everyone wants a hug.

9. Provide hospitality. Offer coffee, water, or snacks. Stay hydrated.

10. Know your own limits and don't be afraid to ask for help if more assistance is required.

Chapter Three

The First Week

HOW CAN A DISCOTHEQUE NOT BE A SAFE PLACE?

In the early morning hours of Sunday, June 12, 2016, over three hundred people were dancing and enjoying themselves during Latin night at Pulse, a gay nightclub in Orlando, Florida. The magic ended around 2 a.m. Sunday morning when a gunman started unloading his rapid-fire guns into the crowded dance floor. Three hours later he would be shot to death, after killing 49 persons and shooting 103 others. Those who live in the area spoke of hearing the gunfire without knowing the immensity of the tragedy until the next day. It is thought that the percussion of the music masked the gunfire.

I received the call to go to Orlando on Sunday afternoon and was on a plane the next morning. The two weeks I spent in Orlando were purposeful and sequestered. The only way I could function was to "stay in the bubble" and not watch any outside news or coverage. I knew from past events that exposure to media would reduce my ability to help people in real life. I did not find out that both the Eiffel Tower and the Sydney Opera House had been lit up in rainbow colors in memory of the Pulse nightclub victims until months later.

I kept trying to find an analogy, a metaphor, that could accurately represent what had occurred in Orlando. The best I could do for a hypothetical comparison was a gay plane crash with the majority of the passengers from Puerto Rico. And while each disaster is unique, as an adult gay man, Orlando felt very personal. My "tribe" had been attacked, and I wanted to do all I could for the community. And so as thoughts turned to recovery of the bodies, funerals, and tending to the emotional wounds, I wanted to be there to provide comfort and help people not feel so alone.

WHAT TO EXPECT IN THE FIRST WEEK

After a tragedy, once family members have been notified, the afore-mentioned reunification and notification center is closed and a family assistance center (FAC) is opened. While the reunification and notifica-tion center provides short-term help, the purpose of the FAC is to help and support the victims, their families and friends, and even the greater community, over the first few weeks. The Orlando FAC at Camping World Stadium (formerly the Citrus Bowl) opened the Wednesday after the Sunday morning shooting. FACs remain open until immediate needs are met, then may transition to an existing charity or humanitar-ian organization to continue meeting intermediate or long-term needs.

Among other issues, the family assistance center helps surviving relatives with arranging flights, death certificates, and more. In Orlan-do, American, Delta, JetBlue, Southwest, and United Airlines all were in the family assistance center, donating flights and assisting relatives flying in from Puerto Rico and the Caribbean to claim their loved one's body. They also helped make arrangements to ship the bodies home by air for the funerals or burial at home without charge. The city of Orlan-do provided free burial plots to relatives who could not afford them; funeral costs were also donated. Florida Hospital and Orlando Health donated all medical costs for the victims and survivors that came in through their emergency rooms the night of the massacre.

In the Orlando FAC, there were also the consulate generals of Mexi-co and Columbia assisting with any emergency visas that needed to be issued to family members of the deceased. Death certificates in Florida are issued through the DMV with support from the Florida Attorney General's office. Normally the process can take weeks, but with every-one under the same roof in the family assistance center, these needs could be expedited and met.

Of course, before bodies can be sent home or funerals can be planned, victims must first be identified. If an ID, such as a driver's license, is found on the victim, identification may be straightforward. If not, the medical examiner or coroner may need to interview family members about identifiable signs: clothing, tattoos, birthmarks, jewelry, and so forth. They may be asked to visually identify a loved one's body. However, after a plane crash or mass shooting, the physical injuries are sometimes so extensive as to make conventional identification impossible. Instead of being escorted into a morgue to look at a body under a sheet (as often happens in the movies), family members may be asked to provide a hair or toothbrush to collect DNA to assist in the identification process.

After 9/11, there was much discussion about what to do when bodies (or parts of bodies) were found. Each time remains were recovered at Ground Zero, a whistle blew and a team including a chaplain brought the remains out to the temporary morgue or by ambulance to the disaster mortuary. The chaplain gave this blessing:

> We give thanks for this individual and that they may be in heaven and at peace,
> We pray for their family and may they be restored,
> We give thanks for the people who helped find this body.

The prayer was simple and brief by design and used inclusive language that all major faith traditions could embrace. Spoken with sensitivity and authority by the chaplain, this blessing was uniquely comforting not only to the immediate team bringing the body out of the pit but also to the larger community of workers and general public.

MEMORIAL SERVICES

Once the difficult tasks of identification and the practical concerns of burial have been addressed, thoughts turn to providing emotional comfort to those left behind. Memorial services, funerals, and vigils are perhaps the most common rituals that occur after a tragic event in an attempt to honor a person's life and provide comfort to those mourning their loss. While some religions have liturgies specifically known for funerals and memorials, community services need to be more inclusive and affirming and not do harm with language that excludes or wounds. Oftentimes, the most moving part of a memorial service is a moment of silence.

One big difference between private deaths and more large-scale events like the Orlando shooting is that elected officials often become involved in public tragedies. For example, in the Pulse nightclub shooting, a decision had to be made as to which memorial service would "get" the governor and which one would "get" the mayor. In this instance, the mayor was the more desirable catch, as the Florida governor did not have the greatest record with the LGBTQ+ population there.

When helping plan memorial services and funerals, keep your focus on the families. Ask yourself, "Who is this for?" Listen to the families. What do they want? Even severely traumatized and grieving persons have valuable insight into the wishes of their loved ones and how they want to commemorate their lives. Some may not want a big memorial service. Family members don't even always want the president or other high-ranking official to visit. Sometimes, a visit can delay recovery operations, so I personally discourage high-ranking visits until all victims have been recovered for the sake of the families involved.

In the late 1990s, when an Egypt Air plane crashed in the Atlantic, a memorial service was planned on the beach facing the ocean. A large tent was erected and the chaplain in charge arranged all the chairs so they were facing the sea. There was an empty stage with a lectern. The chaplain left briefly to attend to other matters and returned to find local politicians had added chairs for dignitaries and politicians on the stage, so that they could address the grieving and convey their condolences. While they might have been well-meaning, the chaplain knew it was more important to keep the ocean as the focal point for those assembled. He removed all the chairs from the stage so that the view would be unencumbered. The officials were asked to take their seats amongst the congregation, keeping the focus on the water and offering time for reflection. The memorial ended up being a beautiful service that allowed those assembled to gaze at the light on the water during the prayers and readings for the dead.

SITE VISITS

Another way to provide comfort in the week after a tragedy is by helping to arrange a site visit. This has become an established comforting ritual in many catastrophic disasters, whether it be a plane crash in the forest, a boating accident on a beach, or a nightclub shooting. Many family members request to see the actual disaster location where their loved one took their last breath. Generally, site visits are held in silence with the only sound being the sobs of family members.

Reactions to a site visit are as varied as the individuals attending. Some feel that there is a sense of closure and acceptance, showing them there was no way that their loved one could have survived. Others are simply still in shock and going through the motions—getting on the bus to the site, taking a bottle of water, grabbing a few tissues. If families do not want a site visit, then don't impose one on them. It may be too painful, and the emotional wounds may still be too raw. Of course, no site visits can be made until all victims have been recovered and any smoldering wreckage cools off. Sharp metal and unsafe areas are roped off and security is tight to restrict the press or the uninvited.

Sometimes it isn't possible to visit a location directly, so we have to be creative in coming up with a meaningful ritual that will still keep everyone safe. For example, after the 1999 Alaskan airplane crash off the coast of California, a boat trip was planned to take family members to the crash site. This was in the middle of the ocean, about thirty miles off-shore. However, we became worried about distraught family members possibly trying to jump overboard in order to "join" their lost loved ones. After a traumatic event, many family members are not thinking rationally. So instead of a physical visit to the crash location, we decided to arrange a ceremony where friends and relatives could put flowers in a basket on the beach closest to the crash site. A helicopter then took the basket to the actual point of impact and was videotaped dropping the basket of flowers into the ocean. In this way, survivors were able to participate in a meaningful ritual while also keeping everyone safe.

In addition to a site visit, the creation of a place to leave flowers, photos, and other mementos has become common after mass casualty events. Often, spontaneous shrines are set up at sites where people have died. Children want to bring teddy bears; adults wish to bring candles or flowers. After September 11, chain-link fences around lower Manhattan were covered with flyers of those lost, stuffed animals, flowers, votive candles, posters, cards, and banners. The site may not be religious, but if it's where your loved one died, it is sacred. You can help by finding out if leaving objects in a given spot is permissible, making sure the items are not in a dangerous location, helping get the grieving to these sites, or taking a picture of the memorial spot if desired. Perhaps the afflicted will want a picture of it down the line but not right away.

SOUP AND A SHAWL
(THE ROLE OF FOOD AND WARMTH IN COMFORT)

There's a reason bringing a casserole dish after a death is such a cliché—it is comforting. I grew up in the 1950s, and my comfort food is tuna casserole. One can of Campbell's cream of mushroom soup, elbow macaroni, and one can of tuna fish combined provides an emotional anchor no matter where I am in the world.

Food is a great way to provide comfort and support in the weeks following a disaster, but make sure it is easy to store or save for later if not needed at that moment. You might decide to give a gift card to a local restaurant or start a meal train online where the grieving can comment or decline a delivery if it's not needed on a given day. And while bringing a home-cooked lasagna to your neighbor is a kind and loving gesture, for a more large-scale operation, food safety regulations make this type of donation impractical. Donating money is a better way to provide comfort in this case. Finally, be sure to take into account culture or religious considerations. After the 2004 Florida hurricane, a Southern Baptist mobile kitchen was serving ham and cheese sandwiches to a predominantly Jewish neighborhood. They had to be gently reminded that Judaism prohibits eating pork. Remembering, however, that food is necessary sustenance for grieving friends and family is important. Sometimes the ease of having a packed refrigerator reminds those who may not *want* to eat that they *have* to eat.

Providing warmth, whether in the form of a cup of coffee or a blanket draped over a person in shock, is another way to comfort. There is a tradition in upstate New York for church women to knit shawls for breast cancer patients because hospital treatment rooms sometimes can be quite chilly or downright cold. So when Continental flight 3407 crashed outside of Buffalo, New York, in February 2009, local churches delivered shawls to the families and loved ones waiting in the family assistance center for updates. The shawls, in both examples, provided comfort and warmth, and a reminder that there were many "out there" who cared and wanted to do something to provide comfort.

I remember being at the FAC in Orlando and meeting Eduardo. The twenty-two-year-old survivor from the Pulse massacre was on crutches and trying to navigate the family assistance center. Five nights before, he had been hiding under bodies in the nightclub, and I reassured him that it was normal for him to still be in shock. Eduardo had come with friends, but they were nowhere to be found. After a quick tour of the

FAC, which included everything from emergency childcare to a full buffet, I brought him a Red Cross blanket, which was quite a popular item in the over air-conditioned space. I spent some time just chatting with him, and when it was time to leave, I helped him navigate the heavy center doors. Years later, I still remember those moments with him and how we had both seen death.

COMPLICATING FACTORS

After a tragedy, even well-meaning officials can make mistakes or have lapses in judgment. In 1994, a US Airways flight crashed killing all 132 passengers and crew outside Pittsburgh. High school student volunteers were brought in to help. However, the task they were given was to use plastic cafeteria trays to take body parts from one disaster mortuary tent to another. High school volunteers clearly do not have the training or mental strength to serve in this capacity! A seasoned disaster recovery official quickly ended this practice, thanked the teenagers for their time, and sent them home.

Another example of people meaning well, but ultimately failing to provide appropriate care and support, occurred after Hurricane Katrina in 2005. Eight buses from New Orleans arrived in Houston in the middle of the night from a Jewish nursing and long-term-care facility in New Orleans. Hospital chaplains at Texas Medical Center were called in to be with these elderly evacuees, many of whom were from Alzheimer and dementia units.

A nurse's assistant had been tasked with organizing medical records for the large group as each bus had patients and residents from unique units in the Jewish home. That meant that some husbands and wives were separated due to their physical health for the long twelve-hour bus ride between New Orleans and Houston. The chaplains immediately noticed that the well-meaning (but misguided) aide had written the number of the medical record file on each evacuee's arm in permanent marker, apparently not realizing that Jewish people imprisoned in Nazi concentration camps during World War II often had their prisoner number tattooed on their arm.

COPING WITH A CHANGED LIFE NARRATIVE

When we experience a traumatic event, the stories we tell ourselves about our lives can suddenly and dramatically change. This happened to many of the families in the Pulse nightclub shooting, whose children had emigrated to Orlando to find work and also a culture of openness and tolerance. Oftentimes, family members of the dead were doubly impacted by the loss of a child and the news that their child was gay. This experience brought me back to my early days in hospital chaplaincy and my motivation for returning to ministry to work with AIDS patients. It was not unusual to have a similar connection: disclosure of an acute illness and the revelation of homosexuality. Some families find their beliefs evolving, as they mourn both the child they thought they knew and the one they'd never get to know. But one body in the Pulse nightclub shooting was unclaimed—perhaps the family could not bring themselves to acknowledge the homosexuality of their child.

For those who survive a disaster with life-altering injuries, the adjustment to normal tasks of living is daunting and complex. Special care needs and rehabilitation efforts may continue for the rest of one's life. How do you reach out and comfort in such a situation in the first weeks after a disaster? In the military, one knows the risks of life-ending or life-altering injury. "Thank you for your service" may be appropriate words to use to comfort a veteran's family for the sacrifices they have made. In case of a random event, the words may be harder to find, but "I can't imagine what this is like for you" is usually appropriate.

In any tragedy, there is a fine line between comfort and distraction. Well-intentioned persons may seek to comfort someone going through a life-changing experience, but instead of comforting, they may be trying to soothe their own anxiety. Instead of seeking to distract someone from their pain, starting a conversation about their feelings may be more helpful.

And sometimes, healing begins when families come up with their own words of comfort. This happened in 2007, when a tour boat capsized in Baltimore's Inner Harbor and three persons drowned in the rough, windswept bay. Two of the deceased were a honeymoon couple, and the third was a six-year-old girl. They were not related, but the two families now had a forever bond, losing loved ones in the same boating tragedy. One might assume that each family would mourn their loss independently. But the family of the honeymoon couple was comforted by believing their loved ones had "stayed behind" so the little girl would not be afraid. Ironically, the family of the girl believed their daughter had not abandoned the young honeymoon couple, so they would not be afraid. Together, these families were able to comfort each other with the belief that their loved one did not die in vain.

WAYS TO COMFORT—THE FIRST WEEK

1. Help plan (or attend) a memorial service, taking into account the needs and wishes of those closest to the victim.
2. Help arrange (or attend) a site visit. Encourage loved ones to take pictures if they wish.
3. Leave a token at a spontaneous shrine. This is especially helpful for small children, who may not be old enough to attend a memorial service or site visit.
4. Bring food. Drop off flowers. Knit a shawl.
5. Say something. Send a card. You don't have to find the perfect words—silence hurts more. Let loved ones know you are thinking about them.
6. Be specific in your offers of help. Offer to walk the dog, mow the lawn, pick up the kids from daycare. Think beyond the casserole.
7. Be a listening ear. Don't offer advice unless specifically requested.
8. Waiting by a hospital bedside for days on end is draining—offer to spell them. A quick shower and a change of clothes can do wonders to help people keep going when enduring a major tragedy.
9. If one day at a time seems too much, take it one hour at a time. Or one minute at a time.
10. Connect with others online to provide support and information.

Chapter Four

The First Month

NOBODY GETS OVER ANYTHING

After a disaster, your identity often changes. One becomes the mother of a student killed at Columbine. The parents of a dead Newtown first-grader. The sister or brother of a victim of Virginia Tech. The husband of one shot at a country music concert in Las Vegas. Victims remain the age that they were when they died—five years old, fifteen years old, forever young—while their families and friends are forever changed.

It's not reasonable to expect everything to get back to "normal" in a month. No one gets "over" anything. There is posttraumatic stress and there is posttraumatic growth. Why do some people build relationships and coping strategies for resilience, while others struggle to go on? This chapter deals with how to comfort by helping survivors learn to accept and cope with the "new normal."

RETURNING TO SCHOOL AND WORK

Returning to school and classes is full of reminders of the new normal. Sometimes classes for the rest of the year are simply cancelled. After the mass shooting in Blacksburg at Virginia Tech, a large, major university with thousands of graduate and undergraduate students, there was a one-week suspension of classes. Classes resumed after a somber memorial service held outdoors on a brilliant April morning. A bell tolled after the name of every victim was read. I was in the quadrangle with thousands of students returning to class but also hundreds of counselors.

There were Catholic seminarians and Scientologists, Southern Baptists offering free CDs and crisis counseling, local clergy and nationally known spiritual care professionals—all offering emotional and spiritual support. A brass band from a small college in Alabama was there to show solidarity with their northern classmates. A bass drum broke the silence as hundreds left dorms and parking lots for the gathering on the drill field, with an adjacent memorial for those students and faculty who had died in wars overseas. There were therapy dogs and prayer puppies, as well as various mental health associations from around the country, all seeking to support students facing a campus that had experienced such emotional and spiritual violence at the hand of a deranged student.

Disasters are really inconvenient. The shooting at Virginia Tech occurred a few weeks before finals, and with only a one-week hiatus, students had to get "back to class" and focus on completing the semester. For first responders, it's on to the next disaster: traffic accident, burning building, or homicide. Returning to work means returning to the next day's shift. But for survivors who may not have special disaster training, returning to work often means returning to the scene of the crime. Walking past a condemned building or a scrubbed conference room may reinforce the initial trauma.

In Orlando, four days after the Pulse shooting, a toddler was killed by an alligator at Walt Disney World. The child had been wading in the Seven Seas lagoon and the beach was completely fenced off the next day. For disaster mental health workers on the nightclub shooting, this new horror did not escape the notice of those working so intently on supporting families and loved ones. While it's never meant to be callous or uncaring, gallows humor is often used to break the tension of intense operations. In this case, a spiritual care professional passed out brochures for a "Field Trip to Gatorland."

After the four Florida hurricanes in 2004, I saw the reopening of Disney World (even if employees were living under blue tarps of damaged homes) as a sign of a return to normal. A new postdisaster normal. The quicker Disney could return to business, the quicker the community would get back in operation.

More recently, I saw a poignant photograph of a mailman delivering mail to surviving mailboxes from the Paradise wildfire in California.

There were ashes where homes once stood, but the mailboxes along the street hadn't burned. Clearly, no one was at home to retrieve the mail, but that didn't matter. Being able to pick up the mail was a sign of the "new normal" and was one more sign that the fire was over and the task of rebuilding must commence.

BASIC NEEDS OF RESPONDERS

The New York City police academy was across the street from the Cabrini Medical Center Emergency Room. One young recruit put a revolver to his head and pulled the trigger in the locker room one morning and was rushed to the ER. He would survive but with lasting brain damage and long-term-care needs. He was a newbie. He hadn't had time to become jaded or numb from the daily murders and criminal activity, parking and traffic details, or opening of a United Nations General Assembly.

First responders—police, fire, EMTs—deal with the pain and suffering of the community as public servants and have a higher rate of suicide than the general population. Stress and long hours and family dynamics all play a part along with other highly stressful occupations.

Adding to the list of duties of first responders is disaster response, which adds extreme environmental conditions to critical public health and safety. This added disaster context adds to the profound emotional and spiritual stress of our first responders.

The stress for first and other responders sometimes presents unique emotional issues. A humanitarian team member from an international organization present in Haiti after their earthquake was immediately reassessed for continued service after he became a little too excited at the discovery of every new dead body.

ARCHITECTURE OF DISASTER

What do you do with a building that has become the site of a major tragedy? For many, the classroom where people died is a sacred space. Sometimes, a decision is made to tear down the building because it's too painful for the survivors and family members to encounter the physical place where their loved ones died. Different locations make different decisions depending on the needs of each individual community.

Columbine redesigned and rebuilt a new cafeteria and commons. Newtown decided to build an entirely new elementary school, finding it too painful to reenter a building where so many children died. At Virginia Tech, the floor where a majority of students and faculty died was turned into a peace center. In Parkland, Florida, it is still too soon to know what will become of the building where most of those students were killed. Something will be built in Paradise, California, on the sacred space where so many died in a massive forest fire. Given time, memorials will arise—from the pylons at Ground Zero in New York, to the façade of the federal building in Oklahoma City. It is helpful to create a new physical place to remember what was lost.

HOSPITALITY FATIGUE

During Hurricane Katrina, a clergy colleague in Texas spoke of being ready and waiting for their evacuees. A summer camp had been converted and municipal facilities opened, so they wondered where were "their" evacuees. I urged patience, and within days, this small Texas town was full.

Then another phenomenon started to take place—when were their "guests" going to leave? The initial thrill of hospitality became replaced with the fatigue of hospitality. There may have been a racial element to this fatigue, when authorities found themselves facing an influx of poor, African American "refugees." They wanted to return home too, but many from the destroyed Ninth Ward in New Orleans and adjacent areas had no homes to which to return.

I remember being cautioned about using the phrase "refugee" because that conveyed some kind of weakness and responsibility of government and was used primarily during wartime. But how else to describe a million or more minority victims fleeing from a totally devastated homeland with only the possessions that could be carried?

Thousands were housed in hotels and motels by FEMA, and weeks turned into months for many Katrina evacuees. Terms like "disaster vacation" were used by critics after compassion fatigue and preexisting racism were given a platform. When evacuees received modest cash cards, there were those in power who did not wish the gift cards to be spent on tobacco and alcohol. In one emergency shelter in California, part of the shelter population was the city's chronic homeless population. They embraced a warm and dry place to stay but balked at lining up for meals as unreasonable and unnecessary. Eventually, persons started to make their way home or attempted to find more permanent lodging and not just a FEMA trailer. Shelters closed, FEMA stopped paying for lodging, and the moment of reckoning arrived.

How do we combat hospitality fatigue? Remember the importance of self-care and being members of a team. No one should feel that they are all alone or the only ones that can do their job or know what needs to be done. All these are red flags and disaster response managers need to be aware of the emotional and spiritual stressors on those with whom they train, schedule, and manage.

Take time off. The more intense an assignment, the less time one should be exposed to it. Management is sacred. Working a crash site is unimaginable to the general public. Workers should be relieved every few hours and replaced and given adequate time to refocus and recover. Do not feed spaghetti or ribs to workers at an air crash recovery site.

Be self-aware and self-selecting. Say no when you need more time to process the event. Do not put 100 percent of your heart into response. Save part of your heart for those who fill your heart or complete you. You can *pray* for the survivors, but you do not have to continually *stay* with the survivors. You can comfort their loved ones and take comfort in knowing that you have done all that you could in the time you managed. Help identify others to provide care and comfort and know when to leave.

I volunteered. I served. I left.

INTRUSIVE HELP

Sometimes, the huge outpouring of volunteers is a tremendous help in lessening the impact of the second "disaster." That is when communities are overrun with press, first responders, and others providing support. But the second wave of public and private response may also compound the disaster and delay vital recovery efforts by siphoning off precious resources and personnel. Those who have experienced and endured similar events oftentimes seek to help those in current disasters. Sometimes, they are helpful; many times, not so much.

After Virginia Tech, there was ample media that was professional, but, in some instances, intrusive. The money shot in this instance was to get a tearful student laying flowers on one of the stones placed for each deceased student. One Jewish student became the focus of a young, passionate, and aggressive evangelical clergyman who would not respect her religion. She later told a rabbi friend that she felt like she had been spiritually raped. Prayer puppies from nondenominational church volunteers sought to engage students with the cute pups as a prelude to a conversation about their salvation and damnation unless they converted right then and there. Pet the puppy and admit you're a sinner!

I find the above examples tantamount to exploitation. It's not okay to try to convert an emotionally traumatized person or community so soon after a disaster. Some will use disaster as a means of extending emotional and spiritual power over a damaged community. This is ethically wrong. My motto for energetic pastors—no sheep stealing! The good Shepard doesn't use catastrophe to expand his flock. Each Shepard has her own flock.

TRAUMA CAN CAUSE PEOPLE TO ACT OUT— INCLUDING FIRST RESPONDERS

Repeated exposure to trauma and stress takes an immense toll on care-givers and comforters. Risky behavior— including acting out sexually, alcohol and substance abuse, domestic abuse—are all prevalent not only in survivors of disasters, but also in those who respond in these disasters.

There is so much residual pain in the subconscious and the need to self-medicate, to feel the feelings or to deaden them, to draw attention to oneself through acting out. Sometimes, the complexity of trauma is underdiagnosed and ends in arrest or treatment. There is so much ad-renalin and heightened emotions—some establish disaster marriages or affairs with co-workers, others have heart attacks, some become obese, some spend the night in the bars.

One had sex on the monorail at Walt Disney World.

Another colleague had sex with their student.

Another had a "disaster husband," whom she lived with through an extended disaster deployment.

How do we comfort those professional caregivers who are acting out? By dedicated supervision that is intuitive and compassionate.

Just as we support our clients by examining their emotional and spiritual resources, caregivers need to do this with one another and know when to ask for help or relief.

During the Orlando Pulse nightclub mass shooting response, I took my team from the downtown Camping World Stadium for breakfast at the Polynesian Resort at Walt Disney World for Tonga toast and macadamia nut pancakes, followed by Dole Whip ice-cream cones and a monorail ride around the Seven Seas lagoon. This morning retreat from the intensity of the family assistance center was both therapeutic and "fun."

Don't forget the "fun" in supervision. Maintaining one's sense of humor in the bleakest moments is perhaps all we have as we seek to understand divine justice.

I'M A GOOD PERSON, SO WHY WAS I SHOT?

What does it mean to really survive? Not only what does it mean to lose someone we know and love in a mass shooting, the question is what does it mean to survive? Yes, you are alive, perhaps with a gunshot wound nicely healing, but what does that mean?

You will need emotional and, for some, spiritual support. There are so many questions. Why did it happen to me? Will there be another round of gunfire? Did my friends survive? What was the extent of their injuries? Who will pay mounting medical bills? Will we be able to dance again? Make love like we did before the gun shots?

Who will help me go to the bathroom? Who will pay my rent? Who will drive me to rehab or future doctor appointments? Who will hold me in the night when I have nightmares or feel guilty that I lived when so many others died? Who will take care of me? What if I'm so overwhelmed with emotions and pain I can't go on? Can I join my friends in death so we'll be together again and be able to dance in heaven?

Sadly, suicides are common after disasters kill close friends or relatives. The impact of one act of violence is transmitted to close relatives and friends who in the irrationality of grief seek to end their own lives to "join" loved ones in death. Two Parkland students committed suicide around the first anniversary of their school shooting, and a Newtown father committed suicide.

Sometimes, there are no answers to these questions. But there is still value in asking them. There is nothing worse for some people than to be forgotten. That one feels that they didn't do anything or be someone that mattered. For hospice patients, as well as disaster victims, it's helpful to let people talk through their stories.

HOW TO ASSESS THE NEED FOR COMFORT:
SYMPTOMS OF SPIRITUAL STRESS

- Religious reappraisal
- Questions about reality/meaning/justice/fairness
- Needing reassurance of God's presence and power
- Questioning the power of prayer
- Feelings of hopelessness and fatalism
- Questioning core faith and spiritual values
- Guilt, shame
- Asking core questions like Why me? or Why would God . . . ?
- Changing assumptions about life and the afterlife
- Feeling need to be punished
- Needing acts/rituals of purification

Religious reappraisal is when the survivor rethinks their faith and religious principles. Someone who has been deeply religious may not wish to attend worship in their faith tradition. They may be in shock and unable to embrace the rituals that used to comfort and provide meaning.

Questions about reality/meaning/justice/fairness also may come out of a state of shock and entail feelings that life is not fair, there is no justice, my life has no meaning, and what is real and what isn't. There is a profound need for comfort and spiritual support in a calm and authentic way.

Needing assurance of God's presence and power means having profound doubt about the continued existence of God and also questioning how could this catastrophe happen by the hand of an all-powerful deity. Comforters need to reassure that God is still in the world and we may not understand the mystery of his power and plan. "Comfort my people" and "Thy rod and staff they comfort me" may be of great spiritual comfort and a reminder that one's higher presence cares for everyone.

Questioning the power of prayer is not at all uncommon after disasters and care providers need to be sensitive to the sheer disbelief in praying to a benevolent Creator that has unleashed such an unimaginable disaster on his people. There are those in need of comfort who simply no longer believe that someone hears their prayers or lamentations.

Feelings of hopelessness and fatalism also are not uncommon. After suffering profound loss or capacity, victims may verbalize negative thoughts of despair and disbelief. Sometimes, one may feel that the disaster is their fault, this is particularly present in children, and that they somehow deserve to suffer. Comforters need to provide hope as well as comfort and discourage negative thinking.

Questioning core faith and spiritual values. One may declare that they no longer believe in Christianity or Islam, and that the disaster is too unacceptable for anyone to believe that love and hope can exist and thrive. There are no "tidings of comfort and joy" when one's world has just been destroyed and everything is questioned or suspect.

Guilt and shame as well as a combination of other spiritual stress symptoms may be present at the same time. Feeling that one caused the disaster by their actions or inaction, or feelings that one is worthless. Why did I move in harm's way, or why can't I provide for my family after a disaster is a very real challenge to the comforter. Giving people comfort, making them feel worthy, and the power of a declaration that "this is not your fault" can be extremely therapeutic.

Asking core questions like "Why Me" and "Why Would God . . . ?" are very normal after a catastrophic disaster, whether it is a house fire or bomb explosion or tidal wave. Taking the disaster personally is unavoidable, and the comforter needs to reassure victims that this is not true.

Changing assumptions about life and the afterlife are also possible after a disaster like Newtown or Columbine. It's much harder when children die. If a victim says they no longer believe in God or Allah, they may also say that they don't believe there is heaven or paradise. Helping victims find meaning in the disaster and their own internal resources for hope and the future may be more challenging for the comforter. The comforter's very presence should be a symbol of hope in the future and that at least someone cares.

Feeling the need to be punished is an unfortunate occurrence in people who feel that they somehow caused the disaster and they need to suffer or atone for their presumed guilt. There are those who feel that an uncharitable thought or act precipitated the catastrophe, and the only recourse is punishment. These thoughts are more common depending on personal losses in disaster and also become a challenge to the comforter to explore and not dismiss. One may need to refer to a mental health professional if people get "stuck" in self-abuse.

Needing acts/rituals of purification. Victims may feel they need for absolution for their "crime" of "causing" the disaster and may ask to be forgiven through some symbolic ritual. These survivors need to be taken seriously. They may harm themselves and even harm others as they seek to be cleansed of the burden of thinking they caused the disaster. Many religions have rituals of forgiveness and benedictions that may "purify" believers at weekly services. Comforters may be aware that the victim feels dirty and unworthy and needs great affirmation and reassurance that they are having a normal reaction to an abnormal event.

LEGAL CONCERNS: UNIQUE TO EVERY DISASTER

The undeniable reality of a death certificate after a mass murder reinforces the trauma of loss. A death certificate may be necessary to access bank accounts and other legal matters. After the Pulse shootings, questions of how to get a victim's car out of the nightclub's parking lot automatically became a legal issue. Who is the next of kin? Who are the beneficiaries? These issues take time and expertise to resolve.

Affordable housing may be scarce before a disaster and even more impossible after a disaster. Legally, property ownership may be all that is left after a hurricane when neighborhoods are leveled. Laws regulating zoning and other legalities are uniquely personal when one wants to rebuild in a flood zone or prohibited region. There may also be Solomonic decisions on breaching levees that may flood areas where mainly poor people live, as a way of protecting more affluent neighborhoods on higher ground. Who do disaster laws protect in a democracy, and is there equal justice under the law? Sometimes disasters do not discriminate and destroy the homes of the rich and poor, but how is assistance determined after a catastrophic disaster? These are important questions to consider, even when there are no easy answers.

WHEN A DISASTER DRAGS ON

In every disaster, there are phases: the acute or emergency phase, the intermediate phase, and the long-term recovery phase. Each phase is unique to every disaster.

During Hurricane Katrina, the acute phase, I contend, lasted for well over seven months because it was more than a hurricane, it was a separation of families, children, and loved ones. Until every child was reunited with his or her parent or guardian, those waiting for reunion were still in the acute or emergency phase. There was no moving on without child reunification even though the storm had ended seven months before. How could you be comforted knowing that your child was missing or living in another state?

Another example of the acute phase of a disaster going on for weeks was in 2002, when the Washington, DC, sniper started killing area residents at random. After September 11 and the anthrax scares, what could possibly happen next to make life more dangerous? When it became obvious that this was a serial killer, the region became paralyzed with fear once again. For those with essential jobs, there was no option but to go to work. Telecommuting was possible although not widely in practice yet. Then the Home Depot by my house in northern Virginia was targeted.

I had shopped in that Home Depot earlier that week. The sniper shot across Route 50 from a dark, adjacent parking lot. A hole had been cut out of the trunk of a car behind the license plate that the DC sniper and his protégé used to shoot unsuspecting subjects, and then disappear into the postshooting chaos. He killed another person later that night in Arlington; not a marginal neighborhood, but a safe and prosperous one.

At Red Cross national headquarters in Washington, DC, children of employees suddenly did not want their parents to leave the house but begged them to stay home during the day because of the shooter. This was also the case across the District of Columbia metropolitan area. Employees were staying home and not going to work for fear of getting shot. The disaster mental health lead and I started noticing the anxiety among the staff around this issue. We met with several employees to hear about their concerns and fears. Although we were national leaders and policy makers, we also were de facto employee assistance agents. We were very attuned to the employee mood and morale at the headquarters and could take our concerns to senior management when workplace issues arose.

Employee assistance programs (EAPs) were mobilized. However, due to the intensity of current disaster operations, few had the time to get away from their desks to utilize it. One counselor familiar to the organization would generally be available in a small conference room in another part of the building and one could make appointments or simply drop by. How does it feel to possibly get shot today on your way to or home from work? Would you like to talk a little more about your anxiety about getting shot? What would it mean to your family if you could no longer work? Or were incapacitated? Can you tell me a little more about what's going on?

EAPs, along with other mental health and spiritual care professionals, can help with feelings and the meaning of an event. Talking is therapeutic unless it's too soon or too disturbing and reopens wounds. I am here to make you more comfortable, if that is at all possible under the circumstances. I wish the threat was over, but until the sniper is caught, I can't make any promises that something bad won't happen to you. I can only be here to support you during your time of need.

WAYS TO COMFORT — THE FIRST MONTH

1. Ask questions about one's life before and after the disaster.
2. It is a comfort to tell one's story but only when one is ready to tell it. Don't force someone to talk before they're ready to talk.
3. After the disaster, only the fatalities are dead. Don't be afraid to continue to ask questions.
4. Survivors may be recovering and depressed. Know when to refer to a professional and pass the baton. Are you a friend or a therapist? Know your role.
5. Comfort takes patience and inspiration. People may not show signs of improvement immediately. Would you like a coffee, or how about a piece of banana cream pie? (Make sure you have a banana cream pie.)
6. Caring isn't a competition. With bold headline disasters there are always too many "volunteers" trying to "help" the survivors and their family members. Best practice: the greater the trauma, the higher the credentials for access.
7. Kindness starts with the expanded heart. Know how to protect yours. Lots of posttraumatic stress disorders are secondary from listening to the traumas of others. Know how to take care of yourself and how much is "too much."
8. Make a will or help a loved one make a will.
9. Grief is irrational. Comfort is dedicated. Be prepared for anything and stay focused on emotional and spiritual support. Make sure one is safe and ask for help if necessary.
10. Loss accumulates. Repeated media exposure magnifies the sense of loss beyond borders. Disasters are not entertainment and broadcasting is not "how much you can take." Minimize your exposure.

Sample Memorial Service

Music while guests arrive: Classical or James Taylor

Call to gather: By a community elder

Music: A hymn like "Amazing Grace" generally is not offensive, but try for neutrality

Nondenominational prayer: May be offered by several community leaders and clergy

Silent prayer (For at least a minute)

A reading(s) from a variety of sacred texts or poetry with respect for all traditions: Read by community or religious leaders

Music: Inspirational solo but nondenominational

Words of comfort and hope: A community leader or one clergy person who respects all traditions

Music: Classical as candles are passed out/or lit

Lighting of candles

Words of remembrance and comfort: Let us remember and light the darkness

Moment of silence and remembrance: Another opportunity for silence and the community to experience the beauty of the candlelight

Music: Classical uplifting sending the community home

Closing: A nondenominational "go in peace" and blessing

Chapter Five

The First Year and Beyond

In 2002, the Smithsonian American Museum of National History opened one of the first September 11 exhibitions on the first anniversary of the attacks. The families and loved ones of those who died on that day were included in the planning of the exhibition and were also invited to be the first to see the actual exhibition. Curators labored over what to include or not include, how to design a living memorial that could commemorate the lives of those lost, as well as educate future generations about the significance of that day.

Even with the best efforts of well-meaning curators, there may be details that need to be adjusted. At that first-anniversary family preview in Washington, family members let their feelings be known immediately and with raw power. To paraphrase one family member, "How can you list the specific number of victims (a number that included the terrorists) on a plane, without considering the terror of the passengers and crews last moments, without considering the intense criminal action of the perpetrators? They should no longer be considered acts of human beings but subhuman animals."

Their appeal to the exhibition curators was heard loud and clear. The story as presented did not feel "right." And so the number of fatalities listed in the exhibit was changed to exclude the hijackers.

For some, that day was as painful and raw as it was a year before. Family support for those who will never cease feeling the loss and grief is always part of the preplanning and implementation of the day. Recruiting and screening emotional and spiritual care professionals—those who have actually dealt with mass fatality and loss—is vital.

Staffing for these "family and friends" events oftentimes needs to be subtle. You don't have to walk through a gateway of ambulances to convey that help is there if you need it. For those in charge, one does not have to have visible clinical lab coats and chaplains wearing crosses and collars. You just need professionals there as a nonanxious presence, to act as observers, resources, and consultants. If someone collapses, there's an available medical response for the physical—hitting one's head, fainting, or just to help assess the medical issue. For deep emotional outbursts or for those who seek the company of their rabbi or priest, there may be initial chaplain resources that can provide support and a transition to the family faith group community leader. Prepare for anything that may occur after the safety and security of those present is provided.

It is important to remember that these exhibition spaces are sacred ground for many families and loved ones. What is displayed are part of sacred vestments: shoes lost, vests worn, hats dented. Any museum or exhibition may be painfully inadequate to ever convey the depth of pain and loss experienced immediately and over time. Having facial tissue is both wise and ridiculous. Am I supposed to cry? Why can't I cry? You should not have to pay to go to the cemetery. The museum is also a tomb.

Survivors may ask themselves, "Am I safe at this exhibition? Am I safe from unwanted offers of support or prayer? Am I safe from predators? Am I safe from those who have infiltrated this holy space and now have intense emotional issues of their own only to prey upon others as experts or helpers?"

Not everyone crying around you is an immediate family member or loved one. The person you may be seeking to support may distract you from your intended client. Memorials can become magnets for the dysfunctional. Preexisting emotional and spiritual wounds can be exacerbated within the general public. Be prepared for anything. There are so many who need help. Each event. Each anniversary. At any time, they could be triggered.

Best practices ask that we moderate our viewing and our exposure to the horrific images and trauma of that day, although scenes at the new September 11 museum in New York City are visible to accurately tell the unimaginable horror of that day. There are marked exits for those who may become overwhelmed with sounds and images of that day.

I may not visit the 9/11 museum in New York in the near future. I taught at Borough of Manhattan Community College. My classroom was destroyed when 7 World Trade Center fell. Even now many years later, it is still too raw.

There are others who believe that it is imperative to nationally re-broadcast the news coverage of September 11 every anniversary so that one may never forget, to stay vigilant and resilient, as well as prepare for what might never have been imagined.

WHAT IS FOUND AT THE CRASH SITE

In a nondescript warehouse building in northern Virginia, the recon-structed fuselage of TWA flight 800 sits. It is a memorial for the fami-lies of those lost when the plane exploded off Long Island in 1996. Sections of the plane landed in the Atlantic Ocean over a wide area, and what was recovered and reassembled is extraordinary. For those desir-ing to view it, one must have a one-hour orientation to prepare for what they are about to see. It is somber and silent, and the reality that 246 people died in the crash is never forgotten. Some on board did not die instantly, as it took almost 30 seconds to hit the water. Many passen-gers were still strapped to their seats by their seatbelts. A student of mine at Borough of Manhattan Community College was in the National Guard at the time of the crash and was with a crew that recovered many of the bodies. She mentioned the corpses had wide-mouthed and wide-eyed expressions of unfolding terror. Is this information necessary, or should one not disclose the complete reality to family and loved ones?

Families are curious and intelligent and want to know how to recon-struct the last minutes of their loved ones' lives. However, it may be comforting to simply say they died instantly and were in no pain. After a loved one dies and before he or she is recovered from the bottom of the ocean, families may wonder about sharks and other predators de-stroying the body. One can simply say that there is marine life in the vicinity. Never lie to a family member, but there are ways of conveying the truth with more comfort.

Sometimes suitcases and wallets are recovered; purses and back-packs that are not destroyed upon impact and are miraculously intact. These recovered items can be immensely valuable to the loved ones who survive. They can also be objects invested with much traumatic witness. Lives cut short in an unanticipated way and reminders of full lives lived or lives cut short.

Sentimental jewelry or a wristwatch can have immense value when returned to a loved one. Objects of great comfort. Objects of great sentiment. Objects invested with great loss and pain. A wallet. A watch. A necklace. A bracelet. Things that they wore. Things that they valued. Things that may comfort even though they are no longer here.

SEASON OF FIRSTS

After that first month, the funerals and memorials (some may be delayed if remains can't be found), there comes a season of new beginnings.

The first home-cooked meal.
The first basketball game.
The first church or synagogue service.
The first wedding.

During the first year, the cemeteries receive regular visits at all hours of the day by families and loved ones. There are times when it just feels right to go visit the dead. Life gets back to the new normal, with a missing hole in the heart of the family.

Death certificates have been signed and filed, wills have been probated, memorials long since silent. Then comes the first baby or first birthday without him or her. Hearts are full and grief is still strong, but we still try to put on a happy face for celebrations in the family.

CLOTHES AND PERSONAL POSSESSIONS

What are you going to do with his clothes? What are you going to do with her jewelry?

These become decisions during the first year and may make loved ones uncomfortable. One of the hardest things to do is throw out clothes—anything that has the smell of the deceased—because another trace, another piece of evidence is being taken away and, with it, the proof that someone lived, loved, and made a difference. Others find creative solutions, creating quilts from T-shirts or ties, donating books to beloved friends or schools, gifting jewelry to relatives. There is no rush to do any of this. The time to go through clothes and throw stuff out or give it to Goodwill is the time when close relatives are ready to take that next step.

HOLIDAYS

That special time of year may be hell for those still grieving. Know that this is an incredibly sensitive period—continuing in a very sensitive first year: the first Seder or the first midnight mass; the first Christmas tree or dinner without them.

We have these perfect images of holidays: Thanksgivings with families happily serving turkey around an expanded table; happy couples sharing that first kiss of the new year; a parent hoisting a child on his shoulders to view fireworks on the Fourth of July. For those who may not have a traditional family gathering after the highly traumatic death of a loved one, in a disaster, holidays may take on a different meaning. There is little comfort in forcing someone to go to a dinner or a party in the first year after the loss of a loved one. It's not about getting over it or getting on with it; it's about understanding that the holiday may be too soon or too fraught with emotion to be actually enjoyable.

As AIDS activist Eric Sawyer writes,

> Looking for an alternative to my reality of my soul mate dying of AIDS at 30 leaving me forever the grieving widow at 32. People wonder why long-term survivors like me, who have buried a lover, or worse more than one lover, soul mates to our impressionable youth desperate for love, are forever in mourning, even after seemingly successful lives.
>
> They don't realize how lost we are, how deeply scarred we are from the loss of love, or from the pain that was so deeply burned into our hearts, as we tried, unsuccessfully, to ease the pain of our loved ones as they breathed their final breaths. Or how the loss of most of the friends from our youth has left us vulnerable, without our army of comrades.

Others find that attending celebrations helps them to move on. When my own sister died two days before her daughter's birthday, many relatives and friends worked in a very dedicated manner to celebrate Sarah's birthday and not focus on the death of her mother two days before. This was a comfort to us. It was not fake or forced. It just felt nice and normal and the way things should be. It was also kind.

There is no one solution, no way it must be. Anniversary commemorations may be "therapeutic" to some, but for others a reminder of funerals or memories of those first days, weeks, and months. When there were so many well-intentioned people asking, "How are you?"

To a spouse or parent, their loved one is still very much here. There may still be many complex emotions a year later in dealing with such a profound loss. Give people permission to share and be a good listener. There can be a comfort in being unafraid to have a conversation about the deceased. It even can be considered healthy and normal. Do not discount the importance of being there and comforting. During these anniversaries, remember feelings are not only enhanced but hiding behind a made-up face and a well-brushed hairdo.

FORTY-NINE DIE, SEVENTEEN DIE, THIRTY-SEVEN DIE

In the recent past, fatalities were described in numbers. Today, it is widely understood that fatalities should be represented by their names.

Numbers are used to convey the immensity of an act of violence, the impact of multiple, horrible fatalities with the name of the perpetrator given prominence. In the past, the gunman would make the cover of a magazine and the victims were relegated to the inside pages as sidebars of a larger story of the tragedy. Today, the victims are given more prominence and the instigator or primary criminal actor is no longer given the prominence or "fame" that usually accompanies mass murder. After the Pulse massacre in Orlando, *Time* magazine put the forty-nine victims' photographs on the cover instead of the gunman. In March 2019, the prime minister of New Zealand refused to mention by name the mosque shooter.

Each year, at the 9/11 Memorial in New York City and elsewhere, a reading of the names of victims is included in annual anniversary commemorations. There is no greater impact or visualization than reading the individual names or displaying photographs of each of the victims. Just reading the headlines of numbers killed and wounded does not convey the magnitude, the human cost, of these horrendous acts of violence.

After spending two weeks in Orlando with the families and loved ones of those killed and wounded, I heard their names read at vigils and memorials. They became real and not numbers. Adding the young ages of the victims of the Pulse nightclub also conveys the magnitude of the loss in terms of lives cut short, lives not fully lived:

Stanley Almodóvar III, 23 years old
Amanda L. Alvear, 25 years old
Oscar A. Aracena Montero, 26 years old
Rodolfo Ayala Ayala, 33 years old
Antonio Davon Brown, 29 years old
Darryl Roman Burt II, 29 years old
Angel Candelario-Padro, 28 years old
Juan Chavez Martinez, 25 years old
Luis Daniel Conde, 39 years old
Cory James Connell, 21 years old
Tevin Eugene Crosby, 25 years old
Deonka Deidra Drayton, 32 years old
Simón Adrian Carrillo Fernández, 31 years old
Leroy Valentin Fernandez, 25 years old
Mercedez Marisol Flores, 26 years old
Peter Ommy Gonzalez Cruz, 22 years old
Juan Ramon Guerrero, 22 years old
Paul Terrell Henry, 41 years old
Frank Hernandez, 27 years old
Miguel Angel Honorato, 30 years old
Javier Jorge Reyes, 40 years old
Jason Benjamin Josaphat, 19 years old
Eddie Jamoldroy Justice, 30 years old
Anthony Luis Laureano Disla, 25 years old
Christopher Andrew Leinonen, 32 years old
Alejandro Barrios Martinez, 21 years old
Brenda Marquez McCool, 49 years old
Gilberto R. Silva Menendez, 25 years old
Kimberly Jean Morris, 37 years old
Akyra Monet Murray, 18 years old
Luis Omar Ocasio Capo, 20 years old
Geraldo A. Ortiz Jimenez, 25 years old
Eric Ivan Ortiz-Rivera, 36 years old
Joel Rayon Paniagua, 32 years old
Jean Carlos Mendez Perez, 35 years old
Enrique L. Rios Jr., 25 years old
Jean Carlos Nieves Rodríguez, 27 years old
Xavier Emmanuel Serrano-Rosado, 35 years old
Christopher Joseph Sanfeliz, 24 years old
Yilmary Rodríguez Solivan, 24 years old

Edward Sotomayor Jr., 34 years old
Shane Evan Tomlinson, 33 years old
Martin Benitez Torres, 33 years old
Jonathan A. Camuy Vega, 24 years old
Juan Pablo Rivera Velázquez, 37 years old
Luis Sergio Vielma, 22 years old
Franky Jimmy DeJesus Velázquez, 50 years old
Luis Daniel Wilson-Leon, 37 years old
Jerald Arthur Wright, 31 years old

One can simply say forty-nine dead or say the names. Always say the names. Always remember. Real names insure that they are remembered.

FINISHING THE FLIGHT

On the first anniversary of the crash of Continental flight 3407, the families developed a new ritual—to finish the flight for their loved ones who perished when the plane came down eleven miles short of its destination in Buffalo, New York, by planning a memorial walk. There was no template to honor the dead in this way. This idea surfaced from the family members themselves who felt this would be appropriate on the first anniversary. They were joined by over a thousand people who wanted to support and remember the victims of this plane crash.

The anniversary memorial walk to the airport also became a sort of pilgrimage for the family members and loved ones of those killed when the plane went down. Memorials, by their very essence, convey to us that the victims had lives that mattered. They were husbands and wives, parents and grandparents, sons and daughters. One cannot witness the grief and angst without understanding loss is universal.

WHEN THE DISASTER IS A CRIMINAL ACT

The FBI's Office of Victims Assistance supports a number of defined disasters, including domestic terrorism, international terrorism, and crimes on Native American reservations. Wherever in the world Americans are directly impacted by disasters, there is a team from the FBI that supports families and loved ones of the victims, particularly in the months and years ahead if there are criminal proceedings and updates on prosecution of perpetrators. Sometimes the contact may last for years, if criminals haven't been caught, or if there are delays in bringing them to justice.

Sometimes there is a dedicated telephone number with updates or closed conference calls for families to use and ask questions. The Pan Am flight 103 Lockerbie bombers were protected by the Libyan government for decades until arrests could be made and prosecutions completed. The FBI continued to support and update the families of those killed.

For the Oklahoma City federal building bombing, the trial of Timothy McVey was held in Denver and closed-circuit television was established with families and relatives in Oklahoma who could not or would not travel to Colorado. These families could monitor the proceeding in private and with dignity and not be doubly faced by the media or others.

THE DISASTER MAY NEVER BE OVER

After the immediate needs—food, shelter, emotional support—have been met, there may be intermediate and long-term needs that linger for months or even years. What happens when one's workplace has been destroyed? What happens when one's home is flooded and uninhabitable? When does the disaster end? When housing becomes available again? When factories and schools reopen? When funds are raised for victims, survivors, and their families? How long will it take to receive the vital and necessary funds? How does one "put a price" on the loss of a loved one?

After 9/11, Kenneth Feinberg became the expert in calculating the distribution of funds collected. He was also selected as a consultant to the disbursement of Katrina Funds, Boston (Marathon) Strong, Deepwater Horizon, and other disaster donations. This was because he was considered to have done a fair job of an impossible task.

There were benefit calculations based upon many factors: age, previous income, potential future earnings, and many other issues. The matrix was complex, and at first, for the 9/11 families, few thought that putting a price on a life could be done fairly, when some would receive more and some would receive far lesser amounts. Not to mention the lawsuits and accepting the terms of fund payouts. If you accepted the money from the donated funds, you gave up your right to sue.

After one plane crash, an argument was made in court that the value of one man was somehow less because it was disclosed he was HIV positive and therefore was expected not to have a full and healthy life span. This ill-advised discrimination was dismissed in court, as HIV was a treatable illness and the attempt at making a "lifestyle" argument outraged human rights and social justice activists.

What about the long-term needs for trauma counseling and help with disabilities that were disaster related? After the Boston Marathon bombing, there would be long-term needs for survivors, many who lost limbs or mobility, as well as those who suffered with posttraumatic stress disorder. Many claims were beyond the resources of families profoundly impacted by the terrorist bombing and, for some, would continue throughout their lives.

A year after an event, many survivors find renewed purpose and dedicate themselves to helping and supporting others. Plane crash victims' families seek to help those who lose loved ones in other plane crashes because they can relate to what others must be going through.

There are those who advocate for hiring those disabled by disasters as a simple matter of human justice and dignity. Many are still dealing with posttraumatic stress, but there are also those who are experiencing posttraumatic growth. Whether it is a survival mechanism, religious conversion experience, or other issue, disaster survivors have unique knowledge and experience that may prove helpful in the future to those experiencing similar horrors.

I encountered "spiritual EMTs" that came into being as a result of a loved one dying in a plane crash and their surviving family decided they wanted to do something to help others who would face the same situation in the future. It appeared that they were stuck in the past, the trauma of the crash and loss of a loved one and hadn't moved on beyond telling their own story to loved ones of more recent disasters. They were not allowed access to family members of the victims because they were there for themselves and their own underresolved trauma. However, in rare cases, survivors of one disaster can be helpful to those enduring their own disaster.

As a friend, I was able to meet with a Boston Marathon runner who was "fine" in the days after the race and had finished the run well before the terrorist explosion. I said trauma was sneaky and that in the weeks ahead to be on the lookout for postdisaster trauma symptoms like sleeplessness and nightmares. Sure enough, these symptoms materialized in time. Counseling helped her, and she is still running the

Boston Marathon. She is a success story because she took a fearless self-examination, knew she needed help, got it, and still runs today.

In Orlando, Victor Guanchez, who worked at the Pulse nightclub and was shot twice, was a recipient of a grant Orlando Fund set up to assist survivors of the massacre. Two years later, he realized his dream of owning a food truck bought with contributions from the fund and was present at the second anniversary commemoration of the attack, serving empanadas and tacos. Guanchez said that he never would have been able to realize his dream without the support for the victims and survivors of the mass shooting. He stated, "I hope they are proud of me." The fund helped him turn a catastrophic situation into an opportunity for growth and positive change.

For years, I ran the New York Marathon, and six weeks after the September 11 attacks on our nation, I chose to run again. The personal impact of that day will remain with me the rest of my life. There was concern about safety and security of the marathon runners; out of 33,000 anticipated runners, only 22,000 showed up. I experienced that marathon as comradery and posttraumatic growth. I never felt in danger and was aware of immense security. It was sobering to see smoke still rising from Ground Zero. But there was no question that the marathon should not be cancelled. That's when the terrorist(s) win, when routines and plans are changed to reflect fear of the future. I was comforted by the other runners and their personal resolve.

THE FIRST YEAR AND PLANNING FOR THE LONGER NEED FOR COMFORT

During and after anniversary commemorations, there will be ongoing needs for comfort that emotional and spiritual care managers and individuals will need to know about.

Not only do we need to know how to comfort but also where we will need to comfort. There have been major population shifts in recent years with massive numbers moving into harm's way to places with more disaster-prone areas, primarily the South and Gulf Coast. For those doing long-term planning, there will be a need for more "comforters" where there have been dramatic population increases. More people will need more comfort not only after the disaster but also in the months and years ahead dealing with their disaster trauma. Every year at the September 11 anniversary commemorations, there are the same emotional and spiritual care comforters that were there from the first days. Each year the families can encounter the same chaplains that comforted them at the various assistance centers in the city and at the memorial itself.

Our nation is becoming more densely populated, more urban. When a shooting or weather event happens in a metropolitan setting, the shockwaves can impact not only the affected families but ancillary victims, too, who may also need support. For example, the small business owners in downtown Manhattan suffered severe economic stress after the World Trade Towers were struck.

Knowing someone has been shot in the neighbor resonates in urban settings. Gunshot trauma in the emergency room may impact those treating the victim, too. No matter how war scarred or beaten hospital personnel are, no matter how clinically detached and stoic doctors and nurses may be, with increasing urban violence, gunshots wound more than the victims.

Sometimes there is congestion or large numbers of people needing emotional and spiritual care. There is a need for more comfort in larger congregations of pain and suffering. We will need more comfort in the cities. Comfort can be found in nature, like in Central Park, or participation in the arts by visiting the theater or museum, or in religious congregations and community centers where the traditional as well as contemporary rituals take place.

Next, sensitivity to diversity will be a major comfort challenge. Our communities are more diverse, with so many languages and other cultural considerations that need to be respected. From Catholic Charities to Islamic Relief, faith-based and other organizations are responding to the long-term needs for new immigrants assimilating into communities in what has been described the "Salad Bowl" instead of the "Melting Pot." This secular example respects essential cultural and language needs and concerns. One can't comfort unless one respects the diversity and brings comfort in a form that can be understood by the recipient.

I comforted an orthodox Jewish woman whose husband had just died in the emergency room. I stayed with her, and she advocated for my presence as a comforter when members of her own community tried to dismiss me. She understood that I was the chaplain, and I was there for her and, for that time, exclusively concerned with helping her.

Those who comfort may experience greater compassion fatigue due to competing social needs versus disaster needs. Chronic homelessness impacts disaster shelter populations and has far more complex comfort needs particularly for emotional health issues. One shelter in the Bay Area of California had difficulties with meal services because few would stand in line for an orderly meal distribution. There is also the belief that disasters impact poor people more than those who have resources. Poor people may not have savings for that "rainy day." Poor people may live in substandard housing that is more prone to destruction in extreme weather. Poor people may have health issues caused by lack of a proper diet and even air quality of more polluted environments.

With social media and continuous press coverage, there is an expectation from the public that people should be helped sooner and faster. Whether it is Twitter or Facebook, catastrophic disasters anywhere in the world can be instantly reported, and people are more aware of the pain and suffering of their neighbors. A social media blast may alert people immediately where people need help and comfort, but what about the year after? There may not be help, including comfort, immediately available, much less a year later. Where is the Red Cross, some may say, when they see the weather reporters leaning into the wind during the height of the storm. In Haiti, before sanitation and cholera became a long-term issue, people were texting the location of people trapped in fallen buildings seeking rescuers.

Disasters also wipe out precious infrastructure like roads and bridges therefore delaying resources including crisis counselors and comforters. In 2004, during the Florida hurricane cluster, Charley made parts of southwestern Florida unreachable. One damaged drug store was stunned to see a drug company representative arrive the day after the storm even though power had not been restored and many roads were impassible. A year later, people have tried to rebuild as best as they can, but many seek comfort in the small rural community institutions like the church. It is not unusual for worship services to be outdoors or next to the wrecked remains of a sanctuary. Many try to temporarily repair their own homes, but it is important to seek comfort in a devastated community's worship service after the storm has passed. These blue-tarp cathedrals bolster a community's resilience and hope for the future.

Many who seek to comfort may be readers of this book, first-timers, who want to volunteer to help meet the profound emergency needs of disaster victims including emotional and spiritual care. It is not only how to comfort but where to comfort those who may be newly isolated, injured, or dealing with the death of a family member or pet. Being there means somehow getting there, and volunteering with a reputable relief organization does make all the difference. Patience and flexibility are also essential, as unmet needs for comfort and support may last far beyond the first year, sometimes much, much longer. Some people never get over the trauma, but those who have been comforted might remember someone who sat with them during an anniversary gathering or other commemoration of the terrible disaster.

It is hard to think about long-term needs when there is an expectation that early needs take precedence. Yes, search and rescue are immediate needs, but a year after will there be those who can comfort those who spent days on a rooftop or clinging to a tree?

After September 11, there were designated funds for long-term counseling provided by Lutheran Social Services, to name one organization understanding the need for long-term counseling and comfort care. The funds lasted for several years before transitioning back to individual parishes in the city and region and the mental health services of the city. There were also funds for individual family members who lost close relatives in the disaster that were significant and could help those who needed further long-term counseling and comfort. But, for Hurricane Katrina, with over one million persons displaced, donations went to immediate needs like shelter and housing and transportation, so there were only modest grants like cash cards instead of large grants.

As I mentioned earlier, disaster needs are growing and that means comfort needs are increasing. What we learned from September 11 and Hurricane Katrina was that the scale and scope of the disasters were beyond comprehension and imagination of any disaster before. Government and the private sector may scramble for enough resources for one unimaginable event and may not be prepared for the "Big One." With the increasing intensity of hurricanes and tornado damage, local support services may be continually overwhelmed with two or three major disasters occurring in one year. The public and private sectors must cooperate and collaborate to expand services including emotional and spiritual care: the need for comforting.

At my address in Nashville in 2008 at the National Disaster Medical System conference, I urged all to expand health and mental health services to include spiritual care providers who know how to comfort those traumatized by catastrophic events. The audience was composed of emergency managers, first responders, and specialized agencies and organizations that may have little familiarity with the clinical training of board-certified chaplains and others who know how to comfort.

Remembering that the primary needs in a disaster are reliable information and reassurance, health, mental health, and spiritual care working together would provide thousands of new comfort volunteers and professional chaplains into the disaster arena and response.

Comfort is needed through all phases of a disaster from the first day to the first year. There is a need for cooperation between agencies and individuals facilitating the delivery of comfort services. Recognize that helping someone is not simply offering food and water and shelter and then sending them on their way. It is important to recognize the entire spectrum of needs from material goods to the intangibles of comfort care. This is what the National Voluntary Organizations Active in Disaster (which includes the American Red Cross) is good at and why they should be looked to as the so-called second responders after tragedies large and small.

Community leaders may be focused on getting public services reestablished and connected. They may not acknowledge the importance of "touchy-feely" things or delegate counseling to others. Leaders must advocate for emotional and spiritual care and the need and value of comforting.

Needs can be prioritized if one would simply listen to the survivors and victims. Using models of what was still needed in places as diverse as New Orleans, Orlando, and Puerto Rico, when the year anniversary has come and gone, will offer clues to what should be immediately put in place the next time any of this becomes unfortunately necessary. Many are asking why? They are also asking about their loved ones and pets. They are asking if the disaster event is over or will there be a secondary event, a second wave of terror. They are asking whether there will be a second explosion, wave, or quake that will do more harm. They are asking if they are safe and safe with us? They are asking for that same information and reassurance after a plane crash or natural disaster. They are asking for comfort.

WAYS TO COMFORT—THE FIRST YEAR

1. Help assemble a visual document of the disaster event (photobook or scrapbook). This may be comforting to survivors and educational for future generations.

2. Attend a memorial on the first (or annual) anniversary. This could be a concert, a recital, a benefit, a scholarship—there are many possibilities.
3. Visit the cemetery with family and loved ones. It's always good to offer.
4. Go on a pilgrimage to the 9/11 Memorial in New York, the Pentagon, or Shanksville. Take loved ones with you and explain to the young people why it's important to remember and honor those lost.
5. Help plan and implement an anniversary ritual for those who may still be numb. Plan a memorial walk or run, reading of the names at an anniversary service, or spontaneous ritual as a way to commemorate a painful anniversary.
6. Help with financial needs. Start a GoFundMe appeal even one year later if necessary.
7. Is it time to replace a treasured pet? Start the conversation.
8. Go for a walk with the survivor or their loved ones.
9. Plant a tree on the first anniversary.
10. Help a child remember and be prepared to answer questions.

Chapter Six

Natural Disasters

In 2011, entire sections of the city of Joplin, Missouri, were leveled by a tornado. As the storm approached, hospital employees dragged patients on mattresses into the hospital hallways and away from the windows. It was the night of the senior prom, and a mother was sucked out of her car while getting pizzas for the after prom party. There was very little warning. There was no place to shelter or hide. It was all too horrible.

That tornado was one in a series that spread over the southern United States and killed 562 persons over 24 hours. There were few tornado shelters that could withstand the immense power and size of that particular storm. An inner wall collapsed on school children in Oklahoma, killing nine. Tractor-trailer trucks were blown off interstate highways like sandbox toys. In the midst of the storm, an African American woman and her family were turned away from shelter at an all-white church in Alabama.

After the storm, spiritual care professionals from all over the country traveled to Joplin to support the community. The staff of the Joplin hospital had to relocate large numbers of surviving patients, in addition to taking care of their own families. Many of their homes were damaged or destroyed in the same tornado.

How does one comfort those killed, injured, or displaced by a tornado or hurricane? While many of the techniques discussed earlier in this book still apply, there are some aspects of these types of tragedies that are unique to natural disasters.

Natural disasters can be described as acts of God for some people, but for many scientists and others, what occurs in nature has a rational, nonbiblical explanation unless "to every season" means hailstorms and brimstone. Floods, tornadoes, hurricanes, earthquakes, volcanic eruptions, tsunamis, and forest fires all are products of nature and may influence climate and, even, wipe out civilization. Destruction from the Japanese earthquake and tsunami in 2009 combined with a nuclear power plant meltdown rendered entire regions uninhabitable and destroyed.

Climate change and global warming have produced more intense hurricanes and storms and with increasing frequency.

IS CLIMATE CHANGE A NATURAL DISASTER?
DOES CLIMATE CHANGE KILL?

There is little comfort in a category 5 hurricane. In the aftermath of the storm, there may literally be no evidence that life existed before the storm, except for a concrete pad where once a home or business existed. Schools, parks, and downtown commerce areas are devastated. In Mexico Beach, Florida, everything was destroyed down to the sand.

The upper Midwestern dream of getting a houseboat and cruising the Gulf of Mexico in retirement can become a nightmare as there are more storms, with greater intensity, than ever before. There is little comfort in exposure to the extreme elements of heat and humidity that is scientifically related to global warming. Whether or not you are a believer in climate change is cold comfort when your home and business is lying in ruins.

I grew up in the Midwest. I was familiar with tornado warnings in the late summer and where to hide in the basement if a funnel cloud was seen. I am very familiar with the *Wizard of Oz* except that houses and beds do not automatically stay together in a tornado like they do in the movie.

In the 1950s, fallout shelters that would protect us from radioactive clouds of a Russian nuclear bomb that could be used if you were away from home when a tornado "hit" were built in many communities.

There were floods in the Missouri River valley caused by remnants of hurricanes blowing themselves out after landfall, but folks had time to prepare and get to higher ground. Old-timers could remember the flood of 1931 or 1957. Now it seems that every year there is a 100-year flood. Levees can't be built high enough or strong enough to withstand the pressure from extreme rainfall.

Floods also traumatize relatives of those whose loved ones are buried in cemeteries where flood waters expose coffins after a severe flood. There is little comfort in knowing that your loved ones are not "resting in peace." Heavier rainfalls, early ice melts, and more intense thunderstorms all can be traced to climate change.

The top ten costliest hurricanes according to the Weather Channel have occurred since 2004, with Katrina topping the list. Harvey, Irma, and Maria also made the list. Just like there are storm chasers for tornadoes, there are those who try to ride out a hurricane with a party and a video camera. First responders have put out the message that they will not endanger personnel attempting rescues of those who do not heed the warnings. Disasters are not entertainment.

Oceans are warming and that impacts weather. More intense hurricanes and typhoons are anticipated and have already occurred. Climate change is a natural disaster happening rapidly in some corners of the world and more slowly in other places. It is scientific fact and there is little comfort in anticipating what may occur.

THE INNATE NEED TO HELP, THE INNATE NEED TO COMFORT

There is so much anxiety and so many citizen helpers. So many citizens who own boats and rafts and kayaks for recreation have now repurposed them for survival. One foot of water and politicians are running for reelection sometime in the near or distant future. There was a peacetime armada in a war against water.

There were videos of catching fish by hand in a living room and alligators floating in the front yard of townhouses. There were vacant stares and looks of compassion and concern. There was a diabetic and a hoarder. A methadone user and a pregnant citizen. There were garbage trucks and the National Guard. There were Coast Guard helicopters and news agency drones. There was so much to be said and not a dry place to say it. And there were pets. A nation's wealth in poodles in puddles. There were bedsheets in windows and evacuations in the middle of the night. Dams that overflowed and responses that underwhelmed. There were people there from dry places in Washington and Connecticut, and people sending love from California. There was pluck and verve. There were many reporters doing repetitions of the same story only different. There were many survivors in pontoons.

There was much information and reassurance. There was comfort and coffee, diarrhea, and soon, pneumonia. There were piles of donated dry clothes and lines waiting for ice. There were so many children and people milling around. There were smartphones and waders; closed highways and power outages; people shivering and those too shocked to sob. There was so much pain everywhere. There were children comforting adults. There was clarity and confusion.

GETTING SERIOUS ABOUT ALERTS

The sky may not be falling, but new meteorology models can predict where major hurricanes are going to make landfall. The combination of science and technology has revolutionized weather forecasting. I can go online and see fairly accurate weather predictions for Orlando for the next ten days, and the same for Omaha and Oakland. Those in emergency preparedness know they must plan for the next "Big One" as well as smaller, everyday disasters like house fires and auto accidents. EMTs need to be prepared for all types of situations and be able to ramp up in size and scale as quickly and seamlessly as possible, as local events may expand and become state and national emergencies.

Oftentimes, first responders and other emergency response personnel have practice drills for anticipated catastrophes like an earthquake in the center of the country wiping out Chicago, St. Louis, and Memphis. These disaster scenarios may feature "the destruction of all bridges over the Mississippi" and the ability of comfort and care to arrive in time to save millions. There sometimes is a little too much glee in the room when the disaster scenario features the destruction of Washington, DC. But these staged enactments are deadly serious and have probably, more times than we know, saved lives.

These emergency response personnel live constantly on call, twenty-four hours a day, seven days a week. Pretraumatic stress may be a constant in the lives of first responders. Emergencies and natural disasters are inconvenient and do not happen between nine to five, but generally at the more inconvenient time of 5 a.m. on a Sunday morning. In the case of the Pulse nightclub shooting, which happened at 2 a.m. on a Sunday morning, there were limited available first responder resources available for those who needed to be called to respond. After ten years with the Red Cross, I suffered from alert fatigue. I could not watch the news or the Weather Channel without imagining the worst possible outcome. It took me several years to be able to watch media without hyperventilating. Even today I find myself limiting my media exposure to the news and the weather as a method of self-care. Speaking with colleagues, I know that this is not a unique reaction to long-term exposure to disasters.

There is compassion fatigue that many experience in the helping professions, and there is alert fatigue.

Alert fatigue also becomes an issue as disaster responders may be bombarded with hyperbole about the next "mega disaster" that will be bigger and worse than anything mankind has ever experienced. At times, it seems like a constant threat. That is why there are so many rehearsals and disaster drills to keep responders sharp and everyone knowing their job and the command hierarchy. Knowing what to do and when to do it and who's going to do it is somehow very comforting. An incident command system details the responsibilities for everyone. By rehearsing and knowing what is expected, anxiety is lessened when the actual flood or hurricane or shooting sadly comes to occur.

One never expects to die in a natural disaster. Tidal waves are extremely rare. Floods can be fast rising but there is always higher ground (in theory). Tornadoes and forest fires all give some warning. It may not be the same with earthquakes and volcanic eruptions, depending on an area's warning systems. It seems like there will always be time to jump up and get under a desk or door frame. Smoke on the horizon or a line of dark clouds can be an advance warning to find an escape route—but it's not always enough.

No one wants their last words to be, "I should have heeded the warnings."

Yet, survivors always talk about clinging to treetops or rooftops, running out into the street, digging oneself out of the rubble, or racing through a burning landscape. Sometimes there are inadequate warnings. Or there are none at all. The evacuation scenes from the Paradise wildfire are incredibly painful to watch as some had to leave their burning cars on the highway and just run.

We are all familiar with the Emergency Alert Broadcast (EAB) Network that holds monthly on-air tests on local television, radio, and, now, text messages. "This is a test of the Emergency Alert Broadcast Network. If this had been a real emergency, you would have received instructions of where to go and what to do." I was in my backyard in

Arlington, Virginia, when the plane hit the Pentagon, and I don't remember if the EAB was utilized in the evacuation of Washington, DC, but this certainly would have been the time to use it. I was in shock when my neighbor told me to turn on the television and see the extent of the attack on the Pentagon and New York City. After calling my husband to ensure his safety and welfare, I made my way to Washington Hospital Center where hundreds of patients had been discharged to await a possible influx of casualties. In the end, I think we only received fourteen victims. My clinical training prepared me to work as a member of a team at the hospital covering all possible scenarios.

PREPAREDNESS IS CARING
PREPAREDNESS IS COMFORTING

The problem is, we know that fully one-third of the population will not prepare for a storm. For some, it may seem like anticipating a disaster causes the disaster. For others, they feel God will protect them or that the government will swoop in at the last moment and rescue them. This last viewpoint has been largely discounted after scenes of desperate people on rooftops in New Orleans after Hurricane Katrina have been burned into the public consciousness. With over 80 fatalities in the California Paradise wildfire, it became evident that first responders can only do so much without the support of the public, and in some circumstances, disasters unfold so quickly and severely that rescue is not always possible. In modern times, no one thought that 1,700 people could die in a hurricane until Katrina. Or that the morning after Katrina, the streets of New Orleans would be dry before the levees broke. Or that anyone always checks for the nearest exit wherever they go, be it a nightclub, movie theater, or school classroom. Sometimes death comes instantly, and other times it comes after spending days in the attic of a flooded house in the Ninth Ward.

So, after the alert comes the next question—do we stay or do we go? And, why are more people choosing to stay in what they know may become "harm's way." For some, it is a privilege to evacuate, to have a car or other transport accessible, or the resources to buy gas and lodging in a distant place.

EVACUATE OR RIDE OUT THE STORM

When Hurricane Rita hit Houston in 2005, two million residents tried to evacuate. Roads were overwhelmed, people ran out of food and gas, and twenty-four elderly nursing home residents perishing in a bus fire during the evacuation. Twelve years later for Hurricane Harvey, a decision was made not to evacuate so that there would not be a repeat of the chaos surrounding the Rita evacuation. But then scenes of trapped residents and a multitude of water rescues from flooded neighborhoods swamped the television networks for days. In the case of Harvey, economic resources did not play a role in who was impacted. The Cajun Navy, an ex-officio group of people with pontoon boats, take it upon themselves to self-deploy wherever a storm with possible flooding is anticipated. In Houston they helped to evacuate stranded people side by side with official search-and-rescue first responder crews. In this instance, rather than becoming a liability, these volunteers were actually an asset, helping supplement a sometimes strained local rescue force. Government, as we will see later, cannot do everything.

Which causes more harm? Staying or going? Often, it is hard to know.

A chaplain colleague at one of the hospitals in New Orleans spoke of the ordeal of evacuating patients from a hospital. When the power was lost, heroic staff continued to manually compress air bags, keeping their patients alive until they could not do it any longer. Some patients did not survive. Some patients were evacuated only to have a "second" death, dying in a distant hospital in a different region of the country without family, without the option of dying at home. The true statistics of Katrina's dead do not include residual deaths that can be related, but did not technically occur in New Orleans. Elderly evacuees died in distant cities. Maria's death toll in Puerto Rico arose dramatically to 3,000 people when expanded storm-related causes were considered.

We know that hurricanes can form two weeks before landfall, but there are so many calculation models for where it will make landfall, and how fast it will travel. We don't know whether it will strike Texas or Florida or both. We don't always know whether it is better to evacuate or whether more people will die or be injured in an attempted or failed evacuation.

And when does evacuation become a privilege? Often, those who have the resources to evacuate do leave. Having private transportation simply was not an option for many of Katrina's poor, without the privilege of car ownership or access to emergency public transportation. This was the first time that it became a significant issue that finances could play a devastating role in who survives or not.

SHELTER

Sometimes providing shelter is a short-term problem: sheltering in place until an active shooter is apprehended or waiting until a hurricane passes and people are able to return to their homes. But sometimes, when housing is damaged, destroyed, or otherwise unlivable, shelter can become a longer-term concern. The scale is also different. While a bomb or plane crash may destroy a building or two, a natural disaster can leave hundreds or thousands without a place to stay. Shelters are for people who have no other place to go.

There are small shelters in church basements and mega shelters in convention centers and sports stadiums. Oftentimes, cots and food supplies are prepositioned before the landfall of a hurricane, thanks to modern tracking of storms. Shelters try to provide three meals a day unless resources and supplies are scarce. Shelters are for the general population and are not segregated by sex (unless it is a Muslim-run shelter). There may be a childcare area and a medical area for those with special health issues. Shelters are often located in schools or armories with shower facilities. The scale and scope of Katrina, with over a million people evacuated, had FEMA placing people in hotels and motels in what was described as FEMA hotels, and, therefore, to be placed in one became a FEMA "vacation."

Sometimes the community donates clothes which need to be sorted and made available to those who arrived at the shelter with only the clothes on their back. Oftentimes clothing donations are discouraged because of the logistical problems of having volunteers available to sort and size the clothes. Generally, there are no laundry facilities in shelters, as they are seen as short-term housing solutions. Also, schools may be closed for students but open as shelters. After the storm passes, part of the transition back to normal is to re-open schools as schools. I visited a Presbyterian conference in Texas that was incorporating showers into the design of new church halls throughout the region, anticipating there being used as future shelters. This forward-thinking group also advocated for having industrial-size kitchens to help feed the evacuees.

Today, shelters have security, because arguments can become fights. The stress of the disaster and the shelter noise makes sleeping problematic for some. Shelters also have crisis counselors offering emotional and spiritual care to comfort those who may have lost a loved one in the flood or hurricane. But it all can be too much, too overwhelming. Everything is different. Nothing is the same. Shelters are temporary solutions to a new homeless situation.

When I would visit a shelter, what I would do is go cot to cot. People just want someone to hear their story, and I would sit and ask them to tell me theirs. Then to the next cot and start the conversation. This is known as psychological first aid.

Finally, shelters must also think about people's pets. I can't imagine leaving our dogs, a corgi and a poodle mix, to fend for themselves in our condo or releasing them outside to survive as best they can. One of the lessons of Katrina was the awareness of how important and central to our lives are our pets. (See chapter 9 for more information about pets and disaster.)

FOOD

Not everyone goes to a shelter after a natural disaster, but survivors still need to be fed. There are those who camp out to protect their property after a storm or return to work on their home sites. After Florida experienced four major hurricanes in 2004, there were food trucks stationed in devastated neighborhoods. Who was served by these mobile canteens? The poor, the elderly, the mobility challenged, and rural inhabitants who gratefully welcomed the meals that were brought to them by disaster volunteers. I embedded disaster spiritual care chaplains into mass care and feeding vehicles very successfully, not only to support the disaster victims one encountered but also to keep morale up for those who were delivering and handing out the food.

This was very successful because for a chaplain feeding the hungry is also sacramental.

Oftentimes in a disaster, during the first week people don't have the option of choices on what to eat. It is still important, though, to remember cultural considerations. In a predominantly Jewish neighborhood, well-meaning volunteers passed out ham-and-cheese sandwiches, not realizing Judaism prohibits eating pork. After Hurricane Maria, and the desperate need on the entire island of Puerto Rico for food, star chef

Jose Andres brought his chefs and kitchen workers to the island and served thousands of hot meals every day in makeshift kitchens and schools. The psychological value of warm food, and the emotional and spiritual comfort it provides, cannot be overestimated, particularly when it includes the cultural menu of local cuisine and ingredients.

Chef Andres also opened feeding kitchens during the disastrous government shutdown for furloughed public workers. Hundreds stood in line in the winter cold for a hot meal.

SAFETY ISSUES

While thousands came to Texas and the Gulf Coast to assist, there were also numerous entrepreneurs, scam artists, and predators mobilizing to take advantage of the extremely traumatized and vulnerable. Public safety must insure that while residents are evacuating, looters and other criminals are not infiltrating damaged neighborhoods and taking advantage of strained or absent police and fire resources. There are those that see great opportunity in disaster, and use it as an opportunity to personally enrich themselves through the suffering of others. There is little comfort in realizing that you not only survived a disaster but were also victimized.

Unfortunately, not everybody who responds to a disaster is there to help the victims and survivors. Just because one is in a shelter doesn't mean one is safe. Sometimes a disaster is used as a major distraction to take advantage of those already enduring immense suffering. Domestic abusers, substance abusers, and sexual abusers all find temporary homes in shelters. Predators and entrepreneurs find much vulnerability in the postdisaster environment. Unscrupulous contractors or funeral operators take advantage of the postdisaster trauma for their own economic benefit. There are always stories about roofers who prey upon the elderly and take a huge deposit to replace a leaky roof and then disappear. Helping provide comfort can mean helping people pay attention so that they don't become a victim of a crime of opportunity.

For those who do not evacuate, there are also major public health concerns, such as when sewers back up and pollutants mix with floodwaters. Mega shelters must also ensure sanitary conditions and not become a warehouse of communicable diseases. Preexisting conditions, such as diabetes and addiction, also tax public health resources, again adding to the complexity and intensity of needs. Imagine how quickly an infectious disease can go through a mega shelter like the old Astrodome? The Red Cross worked with a team from the Harvard School of Public Health, during Katrina and Houston, to ensure food safety and infection control. It was very successful.

HOSPICE EXPERIENCE HELPS

In my experience, those who have been trained in hospice work have a natural connection with disaster work. Hospice workers must have tremendous patience to work with those who face "slow" death or declining health over a period of weeks or even months. Waiting for wildfires to burn out, flood waters to subside, or watching for that monster hurricane to pass over the southern Atlantic, all have time in common. They are slowly unfolding disasters and not overnight "stun and done" events. In contrast, human-caused disasters generally happen quickly—mass shootings, dirty bombs, chemical explosions, plane crashes are all examples of faster death.

I deployed two chaplains with hospice experience to Iowa after a tornado hit a Boy Scout camp. The scouts had just finished eating spaghetti and had very little warning when the tornado struck. They were in a stone-walled building and the winds were clocked at 165 mph. One survivor was aware he was being sucked up a fireplace that was collapsing at the same time. This was a killer tornado that hit in the early evening and killed 4 young scouts and injured 48.

Any disaster where lives are lost creates lifelong issues for the survivors, their families, and loved ones. Survivor's guilt is primary but also a lifelong wondering about the meaning of the event, because even years later, it may feel overwhelming, and nearly impossible to stave off depression. For those Scouts who died instantly at the hand of weather, their day had been filled with service projects and leadership training. These were good kids and even with accurate weather forecasts, one did not feel in danger. Having access to a secure building does not make one immune to walls collapsing or trees exploding.

When a natural disaster kills, it generally is quick: drowning in a flood, being killed in a building collapse during a tornado or hurricane, being caught in one's vehicle while trying to escape a wildfire. A tsunami or volcanic eruption may give some indication of occurrence before it hits, but earthquakes give precious little warning. Some fatalities may linger in collapsed buildings, unable to be found in time. In

Haiti, family members dug with their own hands through debris and concrete and rebar. Rescue and recovery are not mutually exclusive. While trying to save the trapped, one may encounter fatalities. That is never easy, not even for the seasoned responder.

After Hurricane Katrina, coroners spent seven months identifying bodies. When a positive identification was made, a chaplain would be made available to offer comfort to waiting family members. But the chaplains also supported the mortuary workers. Sometimes, they wanted to talk about their job; more often, they wanted to discuss sports or movies, anything to feel a sense of normalcy in the horrific conditions of the Louisiana heat and humidity in a morgue.

SECURING THE PERIMETER—IT'S ALL ABOUT ACCESS

Natural disasters may also be criminal events. Many of the western wildfires with fatalities were set purposely. Criminal charges are normally filed once the perpetrators are identified, which may come weeks and months later, as forensics teams work to find the origin and cause of the fire.

Crime scenes need to be secure environments. Until deaths are investigated and evidence collected, the designated area must be kept away from the general public and press so as not to corrupt the site or the evidence. Most natural disasters are not deemed criminal acts unless you extrapolate human-caused climate change. Because of the magnitude and complexity of disasters, there may not be a "smoking gun" to assign human blame or neglect. With more people moving to southern coastal states and the growing intensity of hurricanes and tornadoes, one can speculate that more people are moving into harm's way.

There are those who "collect" disasters and demand access merely because of who they are. Some may show off their hats and badges and pins from all the disasters they participated in. This isn't helpful; it seems more self-serving. Oftentimes, self-deployed chaplains overwhelm a service delivery site because they feel they have a right to be there, even though their presence is not helpful. But no one has a right to access the victims or survivors of a natural or human-caused disaster except first responders and medical personnel, and, oftentimes, a chaplain who has been sent there from a legitimate local rescue service.

HOPE

So, how do you comfort the survivors of natural disasters? The basics still apply—give them hope with a safe place to stay and food to eat. Give them trusted counselors and, for persons of faith, chaplains that are familiar with the language of hope and the future. Comfort can be offered with the knowledge that there will be a safe place to stay and reliable assessments of needs. Comfort will be offered by giving facts, from which neighborhood is flooding to an explanation of what help is being offered.

Parents and children also need to know that schools will reopen as schools when the need to use them as a shelter ends. It is important to get back to the new normal. Children are very resilient and can adapt to new classrooms, but they also, along with their parents, need to process the emotional and spiritual damage done in a safe place. This may be a shelter or school classroom or place of worship.

Comfort may be as simple as hugging the family dog, who is also welcome in the rescue boat. The images of rooftop rescues during Hurricane Katrina can trigger sentiments buried for years. Survivors will always remember their hurricane, their fire, their flood. A hurricane is not something that one must "get over." A hurricane, for those directly impacted, will always be there. Comfort is knowing there are so many good people united in one effort. Comfort also can be the reassurance that this disaster will end, the rain will cease, and the sun will come out again.

TOTEMS

In the first responder community, there are many traditions. Many unspoken and unadvertised but profoundly important nonetheless. Many spouses may give a bracelet or a necklace that is always worn and not only when responding to a disaster. It is a constant reminder of another's love and prayers for protection and extremely comforting. These are totems and are symbols of a first responder tribe and are taken extremely seriously.

HOW TO COMFORT DURING A NATURAL DISASTER

1. It's a comfort to always know where the exits are and tell others.

2. It's a comfort to always include pets in a family sheltering plan.
3. Volunteer in a shelter or emergency response operation.
4. Shut up and let the silences speak.
5. Set up a meditation room in a shelter or family assistance center.
6. Always ask the choir to sing. Be present and engaged. Use what you have.
7. Start a conversation with a policeman or fireman and tell them how much you appreciate what they do. You might start with a general comment about the local sports team.
8. Help an elderly relative sort through bids for house repairs.
9. Don't misuse your power to comfort.
10. Comfort may not be a big gesture but a small action.

CONTENTS OF A DISASTER KIT FROM READY.GOV

- Water: one gallon of water per person per day for at least three days, for drinking and sanitation
- Food: at least a three-day supply of nonperishable food
- Battery-powered or hand-crank radio and a NOAA weather radio with tone alert
- Flashlight
- First-aid kit
- Extra batteries
- Whistle to signal for help
- Dust mask to help filter contaminated air and plastic sheeting and duct tape to shelter in place
- Moist towelettes, garbage bags, and plastic ties for personal sanitation
- Wrench or pliers to turn off utilities
- Manual can opener for food
- Local maps
- Cellphone with chargers and a backup battery

Additional Emergency Supplies from Ready.gov

Consider adding the following items to your emergency supply kit based on your individual needs:

- Prescription medications

- Nonprescription medications such as pain relievers, antidiarrhea medication, antacids, or laxatives
- Glasses and contact lens solution
- Infant formula, bottles, diapers, wipes, diaper rash cream
- Pet food and extra water for your pet
- Cash or traveler's checks
- Important family documents such as copies of insurance policies, identification, and bank account records saved electronically or in a waterproof, portable container
- Sleeping bag or warm blanket for each person
- Complete change of clothing appropriate for your climate and sturdy shoes
- Household chlorine bleach and medicine dropper to disinfect water
- Fire extinguisher
- Matches in a waterproof container
- Feminine supplies and personal hygiene items
- Mess kits, paper cups, plates, paper towels and plastic utensils
- Paper and pencil
- Books, games, puzzles or other activities for children [1]

NOTE

1. www.ready.gov

Chapter Seven

Managing Comfort

WHY DO YOU WANT TO VOLUNTEER?

Why is it important to ask this question? Because the reality is that not all volunteers are "good" volunteers after a disaster. One does not have a right to volunteer. The more complex and intense a disaster, the more specialized training and experience is required.

This basic screening question should start the conversation which determines if there is a role for someone to fill on a disaster deployment. When screening one wannabe chaplain seeking to respond to a plane crash, the question was asked and his response was, "I know why the plane went down. The passengers were sinners." That "chaplain" was not selected. Out of 3,000 spiritual care professionals who sought assignments in official family assistance centers after September 11, only 800 were selected to support survivors and their loved ones. There were those who applied who said they could only work at Ground Zero, which immediately precluded an assignment there. As a volunteer, you must be open-minded as to where you need to work. Disasters are no place for prima donnas. Patience and flexibility are key attributes that I always looked for when assigning duties and indeed those two words are a kind of mantra in the disaster world.

This chapter discusses how to select the best individuals to provide comfort after a disaster, and how to ensure that the helpers do not end up needing comfort themselves.

MANAGING VOLUNTEERS

Managing volunteers is sacred work. The intention is generally faith-driven and the motivation pure. However, when 250,000 volunteers were deployed during the response to Hurricanes Katrina and Rita in the first four months, a colossal infrastructure had to be developed. For a time, it was humorously described as "the world's largest adventure travel service."

Sometimes volunteers would simply self-deploy and show up at the doors of locally impacted churches and shelters. While well-intentioned, the possibility existed that they could end up doing more harm than good. A good volunteer has disaster training, a basic orientation to the disaster, and an understanding of the specific role to be undertaken. The business of comfort is so large now that the government has instituted an integrated command system based upon a hierarchal structure inspired by military operations. Through national VOAD (Voluntary Organizations Active in Disaster) partners, the MISS system was developed.

MISS stands for:

M) Member: Are you a member of an organization or group? Or are you a lone ranger?

I) Invited: Have you been invited to respond to this disaster?

S) Specialized training: Do you have specialized training for disaster?

S) Specific task: Have you been invited to perform a specific task based upon a specific need?

When a mass fatality catastrophe occurs in one's neighborhood, that community joins a club that no one wants to become a member of; however, often there a feeling that these same people have a duty to comfort the next group who are similarly bereaved. Oftentimes this is not helpful. Here is why. One needs to deal with their own shock and grief sufficiently before they can do more than merely commiserate with another family's pain. While this can be comforting, it is not the same as having a trained grief counselor on-site. This may sound mean, but it is necessary to protect the current mourners.

The implication of loss and knowing how others must feel is problematic. Sometimes, on rare occasions, these former family members and loved ones can be of assistance, but generally, the trauma has been too intense and the need to assist others masks deeper wounds. The altruistic spirit is honorable, but needs to be evaluated on a case-by-case basis. I would caution against sending someone who has personal experience with such catastrophic and traumatic loss to counsel others who have just experienced a similar loss.

It is also important to remember that just because one has entered an official shelter does not mean that everyone there is "safe." If the community had child sex offenders before the disaster, the community will have child sex offenders after the disaster. Parents and caregivers need to be cautious. Background checks can be run on official volunteers, but it is impossible to run background checks on all evacuees. Nineteen thousand people entered the Houston Astrodome after Hurricane Katrina, and to have done background checks on all of them would have put an undue burden on those seeking shelter. Families must be vigilant and not assume that a shelter is free childcare. This is extremely rare, but there are reasons for concern. There are local police on-call, but in the middle of a disaster, they may be preoccupied with rescue and public safety.

Likewise, the need for childcare does not evaporate in a shelter. Parents may still need to go to work, even if the schools their children usually attend remain closed. The Church of the Brethren, whose national headquarters is in Ashland, Ohio, is one example of an organization that provides critical response childcare (CRC) after a disaster. This small Protestant denomination has developed a niche in disaster childcare. Its volunteers are recruited, trained, and screened and can work with children who have been traumatized or are from homes where family members have been lost or impacted. At the family assistance center in Orlando after the Pulse nightclub shooting, it was heartwarming to see that many of the preschool children had drawn rainbows and those pictures were plastered all over the walls.

TRAINING VOLUNTEERS

At the American Red Cross after September 11, I managed a team of spiritual care professionals that I recruited, screened, and trained from a national pool of professional chaplains. The weeklong trainings were held in Pine Bluff, Arkansas, on the grounds of the US Arsenal, a small military base north of town. I trained rabbis, an iman, Catholic priests and sisters religious, Protestant ministers, deacons, and first responder chaplains from the police, fire departments, and the military. People from all 50 states were represented. Training for mass fatality disasters is clearly anxiety producing and I would do team building between mental health and spiritual care professionals who were curious as to each of their roles in a catastrophic disaster.

At the American Red Cross, I managed a team of more than 200 spiritual care professionals who took turns being on-call for one month as part of a critical response team responding to mass fatality events, whether or not they actually occurred during that time period. They were in charge of the religious or spiritual rituals surrounding death and worked very closely with mental health professionals.

As a trainer at the American Red Cross, I found that hospice workers made good disaster spiritual care responders. Their training and experience—learning how to be with persons and their loved ones who anticipate grief—is transferable to the disaster arena, where unanticipated death through attack or accident precipitates unimaginable emotional and spiritual trauma to loved ones of those who suffer immediate and, in most instances, horrific death. The language is increasingly theological (e.g., "Why did God do this to me/us?"). Mental health professionals may not be comfortable with theological questions and might refer to disaster spiritual care. Likewise, spiritual care professionals know when to refer to mental health.

One of the things that came out of my experience with catastrophic disaster is that hospice chaplains seemed better able to immediately jump into a disaster situation and be of great service, while nonhospice chaplains needed more supervision and coaching. Sometimes there are no answers, there are no words, which may explain or give comfort to those who must endure days and months of suffering and believe in a benevolent, loving Creator. It is vital to be that compassionate presence, to know how to sit and be with those who are terminally ill and with those who love them. This is something that hospice chaplains do on a daily basis and why they were such useful members of my spiritual care team.

Likewise, when catastrophic events occur, the same training and experience, as well as emotional and spiritual support, transposed to the family assistance center can identify and access support for human and material loss. Those who have served in hospices are better trained and conditioned to be with those profoundly impacted by these disaster events.

When there were many victims, like in a plane crash or hurricane, I required higher certification for volunteers who would work more closely with the families. Part of the recruitment and screening for disaster chaplains insured experienced help and competency. I was rigid in requiring board certification or an equivalent to insure that someone with two-day's worth of training was not sent in harm's way and might be in over his or her head. There are those with a two-day critical incident stress management (CISM) training that expect to be deployed to mass fatality disasters, but I required board-certified chaplains with a minimum of four units of clinical pastoral education (CPE). CPE-board-certified chaplains generally have a master's degree in theology or pastoral counseling, as well as 400 hours of clinical training and group process and reflection. I received my CPE training at Memorial Sloan Kettering Cancer Center, New York Hospital, and New York Methodist Hospital in Park Slope, Brooklyn.

CHAPLAIN VERSUS PSYCHOLOGIST

Chaplains know how to be with persons of all major faith traditions as well as those who claim no faith tradition at all. Board-certified chaplains have faced rigorous clinical training and small group process to be that compassionate presence while one is undergoing health challenges. Chaplains in the military are trained to be the nonanxious presence on the battlefield. The hospice chaplain as a specialization knows how to respond to disaster. This may not be a welcome or helpful time for a theological explanation or generalization. Why did God destroy Joplin, Missouri, or kill 562 persons in Alabama, Mississippi, and the South in an unprecedented tornadic outbreak in 2011? So what tools specifically does a hospice chaplain draw upon? They use the ministry of presence. Knowing how to be with someone and be the nonanxious presence. Knowing when to let the silences speak and knowing when to advocate for the patient and the family. Recently palliative care has become a specialty of hospice chaplaincy. This makes the chaplain a true advocate for the patient and family with the medical staff. As mentioned before, this makes these chaplains even more helpful in disaster care.

On the other hand, mental health professionals are used to referrals and generally wait to be contacted before offering assistance. Spiritual care professionals are comfortable walking up and starting a conversation. On September 11, there was room for both models. There were episodes of psychologists passing priests in the subway, consoling one another and giving communion.

Mental health professionals may have behaviorial health expertise and know how to refer people for further treatment and medication. They can be licensed clinical social workers, psychologists, and psychiatrists. They must have a mental health degree and license in order to volunteer with the American Red Cross and be deployed to areas of disaster.

No one discipline claims to have all the answers or interventions that will suddenly make everything okay and heal all wounds—emotional and raw, spiritual and unforgettable. Somehow the mass fatalities of September 11 made spiritual care an acceptable intervention for mental health associations which, after the attacks, began adding spiritual care organizations and houses of worship as suitable for consideration for those seeking help.

Sometimes a family member may express a desire for a chaplain instead of a mental health professional, saying something along the lines of "I am grieving. I am not crazy." Prayer had not come to psychology overnight, but religion, for some, ceased to be a pathology. Clients spoke about their grieving and preference to speak with a chaplain. I also had firsthand experience in training all members of our team about the unique aspects of spiritual care and why death from disaster may require the services of a chaplain or local clergy.

COMPASSION FATIGUE

Another study published in *The Journal of Nervous Diseases,* which was completed after September 11, found that having even the most basic disaster training resulted in a lower incidence of compassion fatigue. Despite all the measures to insure compliance, several people who should have been flagged earlier made it through the selection process, thus making deployments more complicated and distracting from providing support to the disaster victims. During Hurricane Katrina, I became aware of a volunteer disaster chaplain who started disassociating on the first day of deployment. This spiritual care professional was a diabetic and should have self-selected from responding. He discounted the stress and hardships of this particular deployment. Unfortunately, he became disoriented and had to be removed from the operation. Another chaplain had recently undergone a hysterectomy and became fatigued on the operation and had to leave. Both chaplains should never have been selected for that particular response operation.

The instinct to help, to care, is extremely strong and heightened by press coverage of the pain and suffering of victims. Is it reasonable for someone ten states away to load their car up with ice and sandwiches and take off for the Gulf Coast while the region is still undergoing evacuation? In the general chaos surrounding natural disasters, the prudent course is to join up with an established group like the Red Cross and contact them to see what is needed.

But we also do not want to exclude others too quickly. In one instance, a quadriplegic sought to be deployed to the 2004 cluster of Florida hurricanes. The issue was one of a hardship deployment including no electricity, which was necessary to support this volunteer's life support and mobility. Instead of rejecting this chaplain, he was assigned to a remote call center operation that gave information and assistance to hurricane clients. Survivors would phone the call center for counseling and other information, such as shelter and food distribution locations. He was able to refer clients for assistance from his home telephone for everything from shelter locations to mobile feeding units. By tailoring what was needed to be done to what he could actually do, we were able to utilize his many skills.

There is nothing like a disaster to bring out the best and the worst in people. Volunteers are there of their own will and sadly may sometimes, just as in corporate America, be subject to supervisors who use intimidation and bullying to manage their staff. Helping others is no excuse for shielding abuse. Sexual harassment is not okay if one is an employee of a large corporation and also not okay if one is a volunteer of a large humanitarian organization. *No means no* even on a disaster. Sometimes micromanaging and bullying occurs and should be reported immediately. Just as personalities may clash, with the added stress from the disaster, and accompanying pressure to help people, feelings may be hurt or abused. The pressure to comfort sometimes becomes just pressure. Emotions may already be raw and wounds fresh from loss of life and compelling stories of rescue and survival. Prior abuse and trauma may cause volunteers to act out, and, again, close supervision and communication is vital to insure the safety of disaster clients, but also disaster volunteers.

Being a humanitarian and responding to humanitarian disasters is altruism at its best; predatory behavior on these operations is the worst, and in some instances may be criminal. Stress is no excuse. Dying to be loved? Try volunteering for one's church or temple or talk to a counselor. Take care of your own needs first before deciding to volunteer.

Being a spiritual care professional means that one knows how to take care of oneself before taking care of others. It's the oxygen mask mantra heard on airplanes: "Put your oxygen mask on first and then help put it on others."

Comforting first responders and enabling them to continue helping is vital work. No one on a disaster response staff is immune from the pressure or the burden of providing comfort. Four days after Hurricane Katrina made landfall, a colleague received an unscreened telephone call from someone who hadn't eaten in days and was wondering when food was going to arrive. After helping literally thousands of people, hearing one voice from the field can be the last straw between holding it together emotionally and providing vital services and feeling powerless to expedite precious foodstuffs in a badly damaged infrastructure. Sometimes it takes up to four days for a postdisaster infrastructure to be set up. It takes even more time to set up services where there is complete desolation, as there was in New Orleans. A good rule of thumb is to assume that you should be prepared to be on your own for the first four days.

FIRST DO NO HARM

But no one is perfect. When I was a youth group minister in a posh Gold Coast parish on Long Island, for an Easter fundraising breakfast for the church youth group, I decided to make bananas foster for 120 people. I simply upped the quantities of bananas and brown sugar and cherry Kirsch for flambéing before spooning over vanilla ice cream. This also is a performance dish and offers the welcome opportunity to ham up the presentation with all ruffles and flourishes.

However, lighting up the abundant cherry Kirsch produced a column of flame that reached up to the basketball net in the church hall, momentarily singeing said net. By the grace of God, the flame was contained and the breakfast went off without further incident. (Note to self: cook in smaller quantities because not everything is safer when amped up to epic scale.) I could have caught fire and it would have been an Easter to remember for all the wrong reasons.

As a spiritual care manager, I always had one nonnegotiable rule among many: respect for all faith traditions and the absence of a tradition (nonbelievers). If you couldn't adhere to this requirement, then work on my spiritual care response team was simply not going to happen. Board-certified chaplains understand how to be with persons of all faiths or those who claim none. Their training is patient directed and not what are the personal beliefs of the chaplain. Disaster victims are very vulnerable and not fair game for those who seek converts.

I also adhere to the medical tradition of "first do no harm" as a spiritual care professional. I echo the profound ethical requirements of "you are safe with me" particularly after a catastrophic disaster. I had to explain this last point to several Jehovah Witnesses by translating the above statement to a more pastoral example: "No sheep stealing!" In other words, a disaster is not the time to recruit new members to your faith. There are faith groups that have strong traditions and feel that disasters and other calamities are the perfect time to convert new members. From religious cults to large denominations, disaster is seen as an opportunity to expand the flock.

DISASTER TOURISTS

Historically, there have always been "disaster tourists," those who wish to see the damage from a flood or tornado, mudslide, or wildfire. They may be adrenalin junkies who are addicted to the high of a disaster operation and the "worse" the event, the higher the high. Some go so far as to collect badges or pins or other souvenirs of a disaster operation.

There are those who picked up airplane pieces from Ground Zero in New York City as secret souvenirs of September 11. Those that thought this was okay may have hampered a criminal investigation. I do not exaggerate. There was a police chaplain who picked up pieces of the planes as "souvenirs." When discovered, this chaplain was dismissed and told he had compromised evidence of the terrorist acts. A brick taken from the Murrah Federal Building in Oklahoma City may seem like a cool paperweight, but no souvenirs from the bombing look good anywhere. If your motivation is simple curiosity, I would say please stay away from an unfolding disaster situation. You are likely to do more harm than good and may even end up needing to be rescued yourself.

STAY, PRAY, PAY

"Stay, pray, and pay" becomes a mantra for those seeking to go to where help is needed. It is far better for everyone if one simply stays at home, prays for the welfare of those so profoundly impacted, and sends money which can be used for immediate needs. Those sums of money sent after a flood, hurricane, or tornado can be humongous. Disaster donations are also great for businesses. The philanthropic efforts of big corporations often can be translated into free advertisement and the cultivation of future customers. This is not cynicism. The Red Cross could not exist without corporate support. Every Chamber of Commerce supports disaster response through donations. The Chamber of Commerce seeks to comfort. Whether using links to Amazon or iTunes, or texting to donate, being associated with helping others has lasting benefits to the company.

For example, Walmart has its own disaster operations center. Home Depot and Lowe's have their own disaster operations centers. They look like NASA control centers. There is enough need in big disasters, like Hurricane Katrina, for everyone both in public and private partnerships. Having ice and tarps available is not only good business, but these big box retailers have disaster response down to an art form. On a personal note, every day during the Florida hurricanes, I would go to the Disney World website to see whether it was open. When I saw that it was finally reopened, I knew it was a sign that the community was getting back to normal. A message of recovery and resilience is when Walmart and Disney World reopen. When Waffle House starts the griddles up, that is also a sign, and a business indicator that things are starting to return to normal. With one eye to the Weather Channel and the other toward prepositioning of disaster needs in staging areas, the public is well served by private enterprise when government cannot meet all needs. Even if the stores have been damaged or destroyed, setting up a tent in the parking lot for tarps and building materials can be a lifesaver for those trying to fix the damage left by the storm.

COMPETITION BETWEEN VOLUNTEERS

On the first anniversary of September 11 in Shanksville, Pennsylvania, issues arose between several major disaster responses organizations that basically centered about signage and fundraising. A compromise was struck where every other truck would belong to one of the organizations. The basic purpose of the trucks was to give out donuts—donuts to comfort.

Help is not free. In a perfect world, bad things would not happen. But, in the United States, disaster response is not officially a government duty. When a house catches fire and a family is displaced, the Red Cross is called, not FEMA. For large-scale disasters, FEMA only assists with partial replacement costs and assistance. Without the help of the government and a special appropriation, the cost of disaster falls on private charities and big-hearted individuals to respond. Compassion and donor fatigue also become hurdles for individuals seeking assistance. Everyday tragedies without a large loss of life sometimes fall between the cracks.

When those large-scale catastrophes occur, large and small nongovernmental organizations and charities mobilize and attempt to capitalize on intense media reports of colossal suffering and unimaginable horror.

September 11 was the catalyst for the Red Cross deciding to roll out spiritual care as an internal activity in disaster services. The Red Cross had received almost two billion dollars in contributions. Adhering to the theory of finite resources that meant that other charities doing the same type of work would not receive nearly that volume of contributions. (The typical donor profile is an elderly woman that donates a modest sum.)

Already perceived as the 800-pound gorilla in the room, the hubris associated with this move to roll out spiritual care was met quite negatively by many faith-based disaster response organizations. These faith-based groups argued that the American Red Cross was a humanitarian organization and therefore should remain neutral in matters religious.

The American Red Cross's intention was to base the spiritual care function on the successful, highly credentialed chaplain model that had been utilized successfully for plane crashes and September 11. The American Red Cross enacted this change without consulting the faith-based community, including the Salvation Army, and the community responded by protesting angrily.

If the American Red Cross became a "full-service" disaster response organization meeting all victims' needs, there was little room for anyone else including the much smaller faith-based disaster response groups. The perception was that a donation to the American Red Cross was not a donation to Church World Service, and eventually might lead to layoffs of faith-based staff in other organizations, which did occur.

With major changes in the leadership of the American Red Cross and other factors, it was not until 2015 when a more community-based model utilizing both community clergy and chaplains working with disaster mental health was instituted. A spiritual care task force operating continuously since September 11 finally was able to successfully advocate and create disaster spiritual care in the American Red Cross. After so many mass fatality disasters and a proven chaplaincy track record, and with the support of disaster mental health, disaster spiritual care became an internal activity of the American Red Cross. The fear that this would bring "religion" into the organization was unfounded after working side by side with the other internal American Red Cross activities.

An example of a spiritual care activity of the Red Cross were the integrated care teams after the Haitian earthquake, which included teams of spiritual care and mental health professionals, case workers, and family health nurses offering services to the families of those Americans killed in the collapse of the Hotel Montana or other sites in Haiti. While I was not in Port au Prince, I was part of the team coordinating the repatriation of the bodies of American students killed in the earthquake from the national headquarters' command center in Washington, DC.

HEALTH COST TO VOLUNTEERS

High-pressure, highly stressful response operations can cause catastrophic health issues among those who respond to such disasters. Those who seek to help have the most exposure to the stress of operations and proximity to the disaster having the most stress. Prolonged exposure to operations without moderation can be deadly.

I lost two close coworkers, and both were highly trained professionals. Susan died of leukemia, and Marcia died of a stroke at her desk. There were also six cardiac events in the disaster response department during the time after September 11. The needs were so great, and the pressures were so strong. Working 18-hour days, with limited down time, lack of regular meals and sleep, eating junk food, and not hydrating, all took their toll.

Let me tell you about one of my dear friends.

Marcia Kovach was an international disaster mental health professional. She was the disaster mental health lead for the Boston chapter of the American Red Cross. Marcia had the compassion, experience, and training on how to support those who have experienced all forms of trauma. I first met Marcia on conference calls from my office in Falls Church and her office in Boston. We were on a planning committee for the first anniversary of September 11, and she was integral at providing support at Logan Airport in Boston for the American and United staff where some of the terrorists had departed. In the days and months after the attack, emotional and spiritual support had been forthcoming for those who boarded and serviced the planes that eventually destroyed the World Trade Center towers.

Airline personnel would remember the faces of the young and old passengers, families and businessmen flying out that morning to California and points west. Marcia supported airline and airport staff, and was also integral to responding to every Boston area disaster, including the death of six firemen in Worchester. There is a haunting photograph of Marcia taking flowers to a spontaneous shrine for the firefighters in Massachusetts.

Marcia and I would later work together at national headquarters after her promotion. We were tied at the hip and knew part of our job was to interpret emotional and spiritual care issues to the larger disaster services, but also to the national organization itself. We took every opportunity we had to illustrate what we saw as a chance to educate staff and bring another generation of managers up to speed in neutral and humanitarian organization.

We shared our story of collaboration at family assistance centers. When a client would start using religious language, for example, "Why did God allow this to happen?," moving a coffee cup was used as a sign to alert spiritual care to come over and be introduced. Likewise, when a client started disassociating and a mental health referral was needed, the coffee cup would move to the other corner of the table. This successful pairing of mental health and spiritual care professionals insured that clients were heard and their needs for comfort met.

Marcia and I could be silly and serious. We knew how to check one another for the management pressure of national response operations where the needs were immense and our responsibilities of recruiting, training, and staffing service delivery sites, such as family assistance centers, were unceasing. I had a three-foot-tall, giant inflatable yellow marshmallow Peep on my desk thanks to my not-so-secret Peeps obsession. When times are hard, you need something soft. If there were working press or VIPs touring the disaster operations center, the Peeps would be promptly deflated.

We cohosted an ice-cream social in the disaster operations center. We bought fresh flowers and put them on everyone's cubicles. When our colleagues were glued to their desktops and phones, we handed out water bottles.

Sometimes, a drink of water can be quite comforting.

But one day, Marcia started to slur her words on a telephone conversation several cubicles behind my own and called out for help. By the time the ambulance had arrived, she could no longer talk. Her eyes were very expressive. I told her we would call her son and daughter and I would meet her at the hospital.

Marcia never regained consciousness. She was only fifty-four. Her memorial service was one of the few ever held at the national headquarters and contained tributes from many of her international disaster mental health colleagues. Her colleagues had come numerous times to Washington, DC, to help birth disaster spiritual care, as nursing had done a decade before to help integrate disaster mental health into the Red Cross.

SUSAN HAMILTON

Then, there was Susan, the national disaster mental health lead. Susan had her doctorate of psychology and had worked both in private practice and in public health policy. Susan was British and had met her husband at Danceteria in New York City.

There was something about me, she felt, that she didn't quite understand, and I felt it had something to do with the fact that I was ordained clergy, as she was an atheist. We spoke about science and intelligence, but September 11 threw the rule book out the window.

I believe it had something to do with mass fatalities.

I have written before that death is more than a mental health issue, and what separates spiritual care professionals from our mental health colleagues has to do with the rituals that we provide.

Mental health professionals generally wait to be contacted for assistance. Spiritual care professionals are comfortable walking up and starting a conversation. On September 11 there was room for both models.

Counselors would retell stories of family members whose loved one was on the 102nd floor and wouldn't be able to get out and how some of their last words was the expression of love for one another.

There were images of falling people.

There was the sight of firemen carrying the dying priest who had been struck on the head with debris.

Then the buildings fell.

No one discipline claimed to have all the answers or interventions that would suddenly make everything okay, heal all wounds—emotional and raw, spiritual and unforgiveable.

Somehow the mass fatalities of September 11 made spiritual care an acceptable "intervention" for mental health associations that, after the attacks, started adding spiritual care organizations and houses of worship as suitable for referrals for those seeking help.

Eleven out of twelve suggestions may have been for mental health referrals, but the twelfth was for spiritual care. Prayer had not come to psychology overnight, but religion, for some, ceased to be a pathology.

Clients spoke about their grieving and preference to speak with a chaplain and that they were not crazy and did not need to speak with a mental health professional.

Chaplains also were not social workers.

Susan helped establish a strong spiritual care presence both at headquarters and in the field for the American Red Cross. She mentored disaster spiritual care and welcomed it into the national mental health organizations headquartered in Washington, DC. Because Susan endorsed working together, it gave "permission" and "cover" for other organizations to consider its value beyond disaster response but also in pastoral counseling and emotional care.

JANE MORGAN

It seemed that a plane was crashing every three months during the late 1990s and early 2000s. At the Red Cross, the federal government was working to provide additional disaster support resources, mandating in the 1997 Federal Aviation Family Assistance Act for emotional support and a suitable memorial service. Since the Red Cross was a humanitarian organization, a partnership with professional chaplaincy organizations came into being and one result was the Spiritual Care Aviation Incident Response Team (SAIR). It was composed of disaster-trained professional healthcare chaplains who would be deployed immediately after an incident and collaborate with disaster mental health to provide emotional and spiritual support and a suitable memorial service— something chaplains were excellent resources for and did not compromise the Red Cross's fundamental principle of neutrality.

Jane Morgan organized this for the Red Cross and trained and recruited its first members and team responses. Jane was my mentor after I received my SAIR training in the weeks after September 11. I came to work at national headquarters to facilitate management of the spiritual care team that was in an extended deployment in New York City after working also in Shanksville and Arlington.

Jane also needed assistance organizing the rollout of disaster spiritual care as an internal activity of the Red Cross, in part due to all the mass fatality air crashes and the September 11 terrorist attacks. Jane was sensitive to spiritual care issues but could advocate for us due to the number of 9/11 dead.

Before changes in senior management and external pressure, and anticipating future terrorist attacks and repeated catastrophic natural disasters, a new template was developed—the critical response team. Likewise, there was a spiritual care response team component with advanced training in dealing with any number of mass fatality disaster scenarios—either natural or human caused. Jane managed health services, mental health, and spiritual care for Red Cross disaster response. Thousands were helped after catastrophic events due to her leadership and advocacy.

I'll always remember Jane calling us together to work on a plan for setting up and staffing 1,000 shelters for 1,000 persons in each shelter before Hurricane Katrina made landfall. The scale and scope of disasters after September 11 necessitated cooperation between federal government and faith-based disaster organizations and the Red Cross. No one organization or agency could manage these large-scale mass fatality disasters.

Jane, Susan, and Marcia were key figures for the Red Cross and the nation in the provision of emotional and spiritual care and managing comfort.

DISASTER FAMILY ASSISTANCE: TWO COMFORTING GOVERNMENT AGENCIES

National Transportation Safety Board

Local television stations kept broadcasting through the night at what appeared to be floating fires in the dark ocean at the crash site of TWA flight 800 off the coast of Long Island that quickly transitioned from a rescue operation to a recovery operation. Many families got their updates from the news outlets. There were no advance briefings. Everyone got the bad news at the same time. There was no privacy or decorum.

TWA flight 800 families demanded that the government do something to protect them from the chaos, and the Transportation Disaster Family Assistance Act was passed and signed in 1997 setting up victim support tasks for the various government and nongovernment agencies. The National Transportation Safety Board (NTSB) became the lead agency unless the incident was a criminal event and then the FBI took over.

Chaplains and other religious professionals are the so-called death experts. Part of the act called for a suitable memorial service, and who knows more about memorial services than clergy? Due to the separation of church and state, the act designated an appropriate nongovernment agency (like the Red Cross) to coordinate an acceptable memorial service.

The Red Cross then partnered with the professional chaplaincy organizations whose membership is trained to work with members of all faith traditions as well as those who claim no tradition. These chaplains were primarily hospital based and knew how to intervene in critical situations like emergency rooms, hospices, and expirations. Most of the chaplain's clinical skills transferred to the disaster arena.

The NTSB responds to all transportation accidents including aviation, marine, rail, highway, and pipelines of significance. They are the lead federal agency for accidents. The NTSB is quite extraordinary in handling disaster family assistance in a no-nonsense way. Their priorities are the bereft families and they seek to protect their dignity and trust. They are a remarkable government agency that works with great professionalism and, most important, discretion.

Office of Victims Assistance: Federal Bureau of Investigation

The Office of Victims Assistance (OVA) is another extraordinary government agency and works closely with the NTSB and other agencies when the disaster is determined to be a criminal event. The federal building bombing in Oklahoma City or the Marine barracks in Beirut all had the assistance of a team of disaster family assistance experts working with remaining spouses and other family members.

This agency tracks the search and capture, arrest and prosecution for family members that receive periodic updates, some for over twenty years. For PanAm flight 103, which was both an aviation and criminal disaster, both the NTSB and OVA/FBI were profoundly engaged.

If an American citizen is killed, whether domestically or internationally in a criminal act, there will be OVA presence.

SCREENING QUESTIONS FOR
SPIRITUAL CARE VOLUNTEERS

Here are some questions that are helpful when selecting spiritual care volunteers.

1. Describe a situation in which you helped someone. How did the person ask? What did you understand to be the need? What did you do?
2. What is the best way to help someone in grief?
3. How do you know when you need help? Whom do you ask for help? What would help you?
4. How would you help someone whose religious beliefs are different from yours?
5. What do you know about your own limitations or blind spots?
6. Do you understand the importance of not using this as an opportunity to proselytize or sermonize? Are you related to or acquainted with anyone who was on this or any other similar critical incident? Have you ever been convicted of a crime? Describe a situation in which you experienced stress and what you did to handle it? Why do you want to work on this relief operation?
7. Questions by disaster mental health: Are you currently under the care of a mental health provider? Are you currently taking any psychotropic drugs? Have you ever been hospitalized for a men-

tal health illness? Have you recently experienced a traumatic event or loss? Are you in the process of grieving for any loss?

A THANK-YOU LETTER TO THE COMFORTERS OF COMAIR FLIGHT 5191, LEXINGTON, KENTUCKY, 2006

Note: While at the Red Cross, I deployed spiritual care chaplains to mass fatality incidents like plane crashes including one in Lexington, Kentucky, 2006. A Delta COMAIR commuter jet crashed early one Sunday morning on takeoff, and I sent seven chaplains to organize spiritual care along with the other Red Cross victim support tasks. There were fifty people on the plane that went down the wrong runway and only one survivor. What follows is an email I wrote to the spiritual care team upon their return home from the disaster. It's always important to say thank you and recognize the impact and sacrifices of the comforters.

Twenty-nine seconds. That was all the time they may have had. You have met their families and friends. You have been a compassionate presence just being there in Kentucky. You have grieved with them. You have protected them, and kept them safe. You have lifted them up when they collapsed—physically, emotionally, and spiritually. You dropped everything in your personal lives last Sunday and Monday and traveled to be with them.

Your families and colleagues back home may never realize just how much you did. Your flexibility. Your patience. Making immediate assessments and developing a plan. Working as a team with the Red Cross Bluegrass chapter and others on the Red Cross critical response team. Supporting the efforts of the National Transportation Safety Board and Delta Airlines to provide immediate services and support to those who faced such catastrophic, unanticipated grief.

We watched the line of blue buses on television and in the newspapers. You were there to witness through your own eyes the final resting place of this tragedy. The burnt grass and broken trees as you held families and prayers in your hearts and hands.

You empowered and facilitated local voices to remember and pray in an opera house for the memorial service.

Everyone said that this event ended the safest period in domestic aviation history. You know what it was like to hear those words, and you were with those who might have heard those words at the most ultimate cost. I can't imagine the unbearable pain.

You now stand with your peers who stood with families in Kirksville and Charlotte, Malibu and Far Rockaway, Little Rock and Shanksville, Pier 94 and Aspen, Arlington and Newport, Boston and Eveleth, Minnesota. Your service was phenomenal; yet, connected to what we all do every day back home at the medical centers where you serve.

So, thank you for going to Lexington. Thank you for being there for your neighbor.

WAYS TO COMFORT

1. Play some movie soundtrack music that is light and uplifting.
2. Find some sunlight to sit in.
3. Help a dog that is trying to sit in your lap while typing.
4. Remind others to take their medication.
5. Silently say a gratitude prayer.
6. Silently give a blessing.
7. Find beauty where you are and call attention to it.
8. Help remember and develop rituals of meaning.
9. Give glory.
10. Give something.

Chapter Eight

Everyday Traumas

PLEASE TELL ME HOW BAD IT HURTS

If someone is in pain, they are suffering. Trauma is extreme suffering. But trauma isn't only caused by a plane crash or category 5 hurricane. Other events, from a car accident to unemployment, a suicide or a sexual assault, can also cause trauma. This chapters deals with the similarities and differences of "everyday trauma" (drug addiction, homicide, illness, accidents, etc.) with more public, high-casualty events. How do we comfort loved ones after these events? What are the challenges in comforting someone suffering from a more private disaster?

EXPANDING THE DEFINITION OF DISASTER

There are over 70,000 house fires every year, and for those who live through them, they are monumental disasters. One may never "get over" the losses from a house fire. When people have so little to lose, a house fire is traumatic because whatever belongings they have are gone. Those who have more resources in these situations are naturally going to be more resilient. As long as no one is hurt, survivors are often told and may also feel that it is just stuff. But that stuff can include treasured memories, photographs and documents, and heirlooms and collections that simply cannot ever be replaced.

There are almost 6 million car accidents a year in the United States causing more than 40,000 fatalities. If you have ever been in a car accident, whether or not it involved a fatality, it is a disaster that never leaves you. The memory, sights, and sounds of the crash are likely to be a recurring nightmare for years. Adding the number of car accidents to the number of fires, it is easy to already see how many people are traumatized. When suicide and opioid or other drug overdoses are added in, the number of everyday disasters or private traumas families face increases even more. Each loss, each event, whether on a small private scale or the larger more public event from an active shooter or climate chaos, needs to find comfort. All are spiritually painful. All require special care.

NEVER COMPARE DISASTERS

There are those who would say that the mass murder in Las Vegas at the country music festival was worse than the mass murder in Orlando at the Pulse nightclub because more people were killed in Las Vegas. Does that make the disaster less important due to body count? There are those that would say Newtown was worse than Columbine because the victims were kindergarteners and first graders and not high school students. There are those who would say that Katrina was the worst hurricane ever with 1,800 fatalities without realizing that more people were killed in the great Galveston hurricane of 1900. That death toll was estimated at between 6,000 and 12,000 people at the time. Or saying the Paradise wildfire in California was worse because eighty-five persons were killed while the one in Arizona only killed eighteen firefighters.

But one should never compare disasters. For someone who is suffering, "their" disaster is important and unique. And as we in the disaster community know, another one is always just an unthinkable moment away. As mentioned earlier, the American Red Cross responds to over 70,000 house fires each year, yet it is the one or two (and in recent years, more) mega disasters that draw all the attention. However, it is these smaller individual tragedies that actually impact communities and families and where support and comfort are needed just as much.

SLOW DISASTER/FAST DISASTER

There is fast death and slow death. Fast like having twenty-nine seconds before the plane hits the ground or slow as when the prognosis given is six months to live. In this chapter we will discuss the less public traumas that people have to deal with.

There are so many children trying to live amidst extreme poverty, malnourishment, or domestic abuse by a parent. There is hypersensitivity and posttraumatic stress, such as when a sibling is killed by gunfire or a parent murdered. The violence experienced is akin to wartime because there *is* a war going on: a war on poverty, a war on racism and violence, a war on drugs, a war on human trafficking. Some of these are historically ongoing disasters without end, but it is still important for the comfort community to try to alleviate the suffering whenever possible.

DIVORCE

When two people get married, it is a beautiful thing—sharing lives and joys, pain and hardships   one is no longer alone. However, when things go wrong, no one gives money to a divorce victim unless there is a settlement or child support. There are tax penalties. Homeowners/car insurance goes up solely because of divorce. There is no small comfort when one feels a sense of failure for being unable to provide for one's family. Add the element of disaster to the dissolution of a marriage and issues relating to death benefits or expenses, and the complexities soar. Emotions already may be exposed and damages of disaster may be brutal. There may not be a quiet harbor in the storm of divorce. When counseling someone going through a divorce, the most important thing is to listen nonjudgmentally. Helping them adjust to a new family situation and honoring the new composition of a family will be a comfort.

UNEMPLOYMENT

Ask anyone who's lost a job or been laid off—it's a disaster—and depending upon many factors, it's emotional and spiritual violence. Add a natural or human-caused disaster and the fear of the unknown is profoundly magnified. Being able to provide for one's family is a basic characteristic of family life. Not being able to provide may provoke feelings of shame or worthlessness. The damage and destruction caused by a storm or wildfire takes away whatever precious little one person may have saved or been given. Disasters do not discriminate based upon societal status or income. Those with resources may still have resources after a fire, though diminished. But an unemployment check is in many cases inadequate before and after a disaster.

MURDER

For a family who has lost a loved one, a single murder can be as stressful as a mass shooting. But the press coverage can be quite different. Depending on the circumstances, it may barely make the news at all. Sensational media of all types of murder are everyday occurrences. Imagine for a second how it would feel to actually know someone whose death is plastered on the front page.

Murder, for me, is not an abstract concept. My friend Connie was murdered in New York City in 1984, and her body was found in a trunk on a balcony in midtown Manhattan. Her death was in the newspapers every day and made the cover of *New York* magazine. Connie and I worked together at Brooks Brothers during the Christmas crush. I had taken a sabbatical from the parish to come out of the closet and ended up at Brooks Brothers (from the high altar to the tie counter). Connie was a preppy redhead from Virginia and had a great sense of humor. It was about nine months later, when we had already moved on to other jobs, that Connie was killed and her boyfriend/pimp arrested for her murder. It was a shock, but the way I coped was to remember our times together, just hanging out and eating pizza after work. I celebrated her charm and boisterous personality and I mourned for her untimely end.

When I was doing my clinical training, a colleague's son was murdered. Dorcas and I were in peer group together during my first unit of clinical pastoral education (CPE). She was from Ghana, and our CPE group bonded over the loss of our supervisor who had been fired for having a heart attack.

We got word that her twenty-five-year-old son had been killed in Japan where he had been working during the big earthquake of 1995. To lose a son in a natural disaster is bad enough, but upon further investigation, authorities told her that her son had committed suicide. He was six feet tall and was found hanging from a five-foot bridge. It cost $12,000 to ship his body back to the States for burial, and a wealthy classmate of ours paid the entire cost. Rumor had it that he had been killed by a Japanese mob during the chaos of a natural disaster. Just when you thought it couldn't get more complex.

It highlighted the art and science of pastoral counseling. You do not want to force someone to talk before they are ready. So in our group we let her share memories of her son and his childhood and just let her process through her grief. It was because of our support that she completed the course and did not drop out despite her overwhelming sadness. We all prayed and listened and cried together, and somehow this awful experience probably led to us becoming better at our jobs.

SEXUAL ABUSE

Trauma humanizes us. Just like my friend Dorcas became a more empathetic chaplain because of her son's death, I probably came to be more empathetic because of an incident that happened in my teen years.

When I was fifteen years old, I was asked by a teacher to help count money for a fundraiser after school. We sat side by side with piles of coins to be wrapped and counted. The table covered our laps. He unzipped and put my hand on his erect penis. I kept moving my hand away. He kept putting it back.

That year, I missed 30 days of school out of 180 and did everything I could to get attention. Even while not aware of the underlying motivation, the emotional pain surfaced in chronic tardiness for marching band in the morning. I caught sinus infection after sinus infection. The day I was to be admitted to the National Honor Society, the principal withdrew my name and initiated a "better behaved" student. The same thing happened to me for the American Legion's Boy State conference where, because of my absenteeism and acting out, I was summarily dropped. Did the principal have any awareness or training on how to deal with a sexual predator on the high school faculty? Did nobody notice that my behavior had taken a serious turn for the worse?

I took all that anger to college and excelled, in part, to get my parents to notice me. Then I went on to Yale Divinity School, where closeted faculty sought disciples to share sacred intimacy. Helping others can become a distraction for not taking care of oneself. What is past is past until it resurfaces again and again. In other words, it never passes. After the Age of Aquarius and before the Age of Consent, with the Vietnam War going on, King and Kennedy being assassinated, and a world gone crazy, whom could I tell? Whom could I talk to? After all, I thought I had been an equal participant. My shame was my own. It was 1968.

Back at my fortieth high school reunion, I reconnected with my old classmates and my old rock band reunited and played great therapeutic rock and roll. I was able to directly ask a classmate why he had been so mean to me and discovered that he had also been abused by the same teacher. I thought I was the only one. Even after forty years, it was so good to talk.

Now when I am assessing the behavior of teenagers, I am cognizant that they may have experienced some form of abuse. My own experience and learning from my friend that we were not alone has definitely deepened by empathy for kids who are deemed troubled.

MATTHEW SHEPARD

Sometimes a murder becomes a national headline. The killing of Matthew Shepard was a major disaster to the gay community and to human rights everywhere. Beaten by two young men he met in a pool hall, they used the "gay panic defense" and left him tied to a rail fence on a hill overlooking Laramie. Shepard did not die immediately. He died a day later in the hospital. He had been taken there after being found hours later after being exposed to the frigid January weather.

I had the privilege of taking a group of hospital chaplains to that hillside in Wyoming several years after Shepard's murder. We were meeting at a conference in Denver. On the bus ride, I was able to play a videotape listing all the victims of hate crimes. I also broadcast a segment from Disney's *Tarzan*, when the young boy realizes that he is different from the apes that had raised him and sings a song about being different. Being different sometimes leads to disaster. Being different sometimes leads to a crime.

After visiting the hill above Laramie, we met for reflection at the Episcopal Student Center at the University of Wyoming there, with the hospital chaplain who had been supporting Matthew Shepard's mother and father. How do you comfort someone whose son has just been savagely beaten and is on the verge of death and then dies?

There was a national and international outpouring of love and support for Matthew and his family after news of the murder hit the news. Though not able to reverse the outcome of death, his parents found some comfort in all the heartfelt messages, even though they could not take away the grief.

UNEXPECTED (ACCIDENTAL) DEATH

Children are not supposed to die before their parents. It's not the natural order of things. But it happens more than one likes to imagine, and when it does, parents and families are in great need of comfort.

Once, I was called at 4 a.m. by parents wanting a blessing for their baby, who had been stillborn at twenty-four weeks. I did not know if they had other children or if this was their only child. I asked to hold the baby. It felt like I was holding only blankets as I said a blessing and prayer for their child. When I was done, they asked if I could stay with their baby for a while. No other family members would be coming to the hospital that night, and it was hard for them to leave the body. Of course, I agreed. This couple was deeply religious, and for them, the baby's death had been God's will. Even in their grief, they found comfort in this belief.

I was told another story, about a young clergyman and his wife who had just had their first baby. It was during the midst of winter in the countryside. They had settled near the family farm and he had begun preaching in the neighborhood church. As children, the minister and his brothers used to play in the creek that cut through the pasture. Anxious to get home to his wife and new baby, he took a shortcut across the frozen creek, but the ice was weak in places and the young clergyman fell through the ice and drowned.

At his funeral the next day, the visiting bishop decided to start with the hymn, "Shall We Gather at the River." While no offense was intended, the careless choice of hymn harmed instead of comforted. The grief-stricken wife never set foot within a church again. Good intentions but poor execution.

WHEN SOME SURVIVE

When American Airlines flight 1198 was landing during a rainstorm in Little Rock, it slid to the end of the runway and partially collapsed over an embankment. There were fatalities and injuries, and survivors were taken to six area hospitals, but many passengers simply got off the plane and walked or caught a ride home.

Authorities had a hard time tracking down the survivors and the whereabouts of all the passengers, not knowing whether they had escaped safely or were lying injured somewhere in the vicinity during the darkness and the storm.

Although passengers may have escaped physical wounds, surviving an air crash is something that stays with you. Whether a United DC-10 crash landing in Sioux Falls, South Dakota, or an Asiana 777 in San Francisco, the psychology of survival and the meaning of the event becomes a part of one's biography.

The survivors of the Miracle on the Hudson in New York had some bruises and aches and pains, but for the most part, hypothermia from standing in the frigid waters until rescue was the primary diagnosis. Later that evening many chose to fly on to Charlotte to be with loved ones and finish the trip. Can you imagine getting back on an airplane the same day you crash landed in one? Many did because they were reassured that the crash had a plausible explanation—a bird strike that shut down both engines—and that their air safety was assured.

A colleague stayed with survivors both on the warming bus on the Hudson waterfront and later at the Marriot at LaGuardia where they were having dinner and awaiting the flight. He observed that most were eating alone and that the dining room was quiet and reflective. He thought it was remarkable that none of them appeared to commiserate with each other. It appears the best course of action to them was getting back on a plane with the promise that within hours one would be in loved ones' arms. And that was a comfort.

When I read about any new airline crash or problem, I think about the family members of Malaysian Airlines flight 307; five years after the disappearance of the plane, no wreckage has been found in the entire Indian Ocean. Regularly scheduled updates on the search, as well as a continued search, can assist families, and financial support can be of some comfort, but until one knows what actually happened, there can be no peace of mind.

DEATH OF A PET

In the Western world, pets are now considered members of the family. Feeding and caring for pets is now a billion-dollar industry. Emotional support dogs and therapy dogs are now regular presences on airliners and in restaurants. Animal cruelty is punished severely.

When a beloved pet dies, it can also be a trauma. I know this first-hand. We used to have three dogs: Hazel, a bichon mix; Sherman, a poodle mix; and Woody, a Welsh corgi. Woody needed insulin shots twice a day. One weekend we were going out of town and needed someone to watch them, so we asked our neighbor, Chuck. He was a little anxious about giving Woody injections, but we were able to explain to him everything he needed to do.

When we returned Monday morning from our weekend trip, we called Chuck from the airport and he told us that Woody was "missing." Chuck had been unable to find him in the garden the night before, and since the garden was fenced, and the other two dogs were inside, he had gone home. After taking a cab home, we met Chuck and went into the fenced backyard garden.

We found Woody floating in the koi pond. I jumped in and picked Woody up in my arms and sat in a chair deeply weeping.

We invited Chuck to dinner that night at the house and reassured him that it had been an accident and that nothing may have prevented what occurred. Maybe Woody had a heart seizure and fell into the pond. Maybe as an elderly dog, he just didn't see well enough at night and slipped into the water. We wanted to make sure Chuck knew that we didn't blame him and were concerned with his welfare, his trauma as well as our own.

WHAT WOULD IT MEAN FOR YOU TO NOT GET BETTER?

In 1994, I gave up my modeling career and started taking clinical and pastoral education and became a chaplain. This was at the height of the AIDS epidemic. An "out" chaplain was still pretty much a novelty at the time, and after I completed training, I was hired to work on the AIDS unit at Cabrini Medical Center, in part to support GLBTQ+ patients. Cabrini and its hospice allowed pets in patients' rooms. The presence of these pets helped the chronically ill feel less pain, improved appetites, and helped to lower their anxiety levels. The pets offered unconditional love. (Walking them was left to me and the other chaplains.)

We came up with innovative ways to comfort those who were not responding to treatment and were at the end of their lives. Celebrating Christmas in July with a scrawny pine branch tree with a patient is a memory I will always treasure. I produced World AIDS Day celebrations and brought in Broadway stars to sing. There were weekly Protestant services for the patients held by staff in the Cabrini chapel. There were Catholic services daily and a rabbi on-call.

At the Cabrini Hospice, it was a comfort to help patients with "unfinished business." If there were any family matters or pressing concerns before one died, it was important to start the conversation. *What would it mean for you to not get better? Do you have any unresolved issues that might be worrying one at the end of life?*

AND, I MISS TOMMY — HE WAS MY BROTHER

What was my "qualifier" for disaster chaplaincy? The AIDS pandemic.

I loved Cabrini, now closed, because a core group of dedicated elderly Italian Catholic nuns were one of the first hospitals to admit AIDS patients even before the world knew what it was. This was a time of not touching door handles or using public water fountains. In those first years, thousands would die in New York hospitals, including Cabrini. It was also a time for staff support groups who were dealing with the emotional impact of daily fatalities and "failure to thrive." Oftentimes, the professional intersected the personal, as sometimes I would walk into a room and recognize the patient as someone I knew. I met my husband through a couple who were living with HIV/AIDS who are alive today through treatment advances and life-saving research. I also came out at a time when sex could mean death. I remember the dead and perpetual grief. There was little comfort being a gay man in New York City during the 1980s and early 1990s.

I lost my best friend Tommy.

Tommy died in 1991 after working as a professional photographer in New York City. Tommy was from Warren, Arkansas, the pink tomato capital of the world. Tommy's mother, Manette, would FedEx tomatoes to him and at least half of them would survive whole and the other's would immediately go into a vodka sauce. On one of his last hospitalizations at St. Luke's Roosevelt Hospital, he swung his legs over the side of the bed and started singing, "Just two little girls from Little Rock," and those assembled would all crack up with laughter.

Tommy would share a house on Fire Island every summer. In The Pines and Cherry Grove, renters and owners started to die and houses sold, and each summer would end with a huge dance on the beach and then sadness. There was just so much grief and suffering.

I didn't realize that Tommy was sick. I really couldn't imagine anyone who was such a close friend, good person, and so informed and intelligent being infected. Yes, my florist had died, and my barber, too, and every week the *Times* had the obituary of someone famous that had died of pneumonia or lung cancer. But that was understandable as a way for the families and loved ones to "save face" from the stigma of acquiring and dying of HIV/AIDS. And they were *other* people. One afternoon I saw medicine bottles under Tommy's nightstand and I finally got it. It was still extremely difficult to talk about because there were all these complex feelings about not giving up hope and the overwhelming reality that he might soon die.

Hospitals came into being through religious groups who believed in the mission to care, heal, nourish, and comfort the sick and dying, to have mercy on those in need, and work for justice, social justice in this case, for those who died before a treatment, vaccine, or cure could be found. Think about what they could have contributed to benefit all mankind and the quality of life and collected wisdom for all of us. Tommy was such a beautiful soul; I miss him, and his generous spirit that keeps his memory whole. Just because you're dead, doesn't mean you're not here.

We are comforted by the memory of those who died too soon, and that memory empowers us to continue to comfort others and model that comfort for those who came after and those who survived.

WHAT WOULD IT MEAN FOR YOU TO LIVE?

In 1996, protease inhibitors arrived and patient outcomes changed, with much greater chances not only of survival, but for a normal life span. These new AIDS treatments suddenly gave hope and turned an acute illness into a chronic one.

Can you imagine the power of this? Before, the diagnosis of HIV/AIDS had been a death sentence, and now, with treatment, there was the promise of a full life. There had been an entire generation of gay men who had been wiped out between 1981 and 1996—the Dark Ages—because treatment wasn't yet available that would lessen toxicity or create a whole legion of other medical issues/outcomes. AZT, for some activists, was poison, and there were AIDS denialists who argued against basic science as to the cause of the virus and its origin.

Hope was found in action and ACT UP and other gay rights organizations that helped accelerate research and treatment and approval of new medicines. Some industries had been devastated—including the fashion industry—and there were fundraisers and benefits in memory of so many of my co-workers, colleagues, and friends. At New York Hospital, when one went in for blood work or medical appointments, the waiting room had fresh orchids donated by the fashion designer Bill Blass to create beauty and counter anxiety for those waiting to hear their test results.

There were support groups for physicians, nurses, social workers, chaplains, and other staff dealing with the weekly loss of their patients. Only comfort care could be provided at the end and the accumulated death toll had an effect. For those who lived through that era, there was PTSD and emotional and spiritual damage. But this is not the exclusive domain of those lost to AIDS. Recitation of the names of those lost is a major part of the 9/11 memorial each year, and mourners look for the names of those they know at the Vietnam veterans memorial. In the Jewish religion, the names of those who have died are called out on the anniversary of their death.

I remember those I personally lost during that time:

James Beran
Tommy Carraway
Stuart Greenspan
Bill Wingfield
Ben Bencini
Yanni "Haircuts"
"Florist" 30 West
Serge "Glorious Food"
"Florida Mag" Craig
Palm Beach "Liar"
Frank Moore
"TWA" Milan
"CK Underwear" Milan
Richard Bruce
"Episcopal Priest" DC
Robert Woolley
Gabriel S.
Ken Reichley
Herb Ritts

Robert Metzger
Michael Palm
Steven Romero
Mitchell Price
Oren M.
Paul Douglas
Dan Taylor
Joe Hartney
Tim Clement
Bob Hattoy

Writing their names— —even years later—is a way to provide comfort to ourselves and others. To quote Thomas Campbell, "To live in the hearts we leave behind is not to die but to live forever."

HOW EVERYDAY TRAUMA PLAYS INTO LARGER-SCALE DISASTERS

There is a higher incidence of domestic violence and other forms of violence against humans and pets after a disaster. The complexity of disasters may add stressors as the cause, but that does not honor or respect individual incidents. Note the recent suicide of a Newtown father and two Parkland high school survivors and the rash of suicides linked to the lack of services in Puerto Rico after Hurricane Maria. Deep, unresolved grief resulting in death coming even months or years after initial trauma only highlights how fragile the recovery can be.

Large-scale disasters, including terrorism, enhance feelings of help-lessness. Individuals are more prone to acting out with a high incidence of sexually transmitted diseases, depression, posttraumatic stress, and, again, domestic violence. These disasters create immense mental and spiritual care needs that generally are unmet or delayed across an entire generation of the impacted.

After the catastrophe has "ended," there will often be a second wave of abuse and violence. Building relationships before the disaster and strengthening family coping skills and community resilience will mediate the impact of both everyday disasters and catastrophic events.

Being on the lookout for that one alienated student and following "if you see something, say something," has time and time again prevented school shootings and bombing plots. One does not have the luxury of "minding one's own business" in modern society. Family engagement—however that family is defined—is key to awareness and turning small comforts into larger-scale community emotional wellness.

WAYS TO COMFORT

1. Take care of yourself.
2. Be part of a team of comforters assessing your community's emotional health.
3. You don't have to comfort everybody.
4. Be curious *and* respectful.
5. Give affirmations to others who may be comforters.
6. Take time to remember special people in your life.
7. Never lose your sense of awe and wonder, as it will lift your emotions and spirits.
8. Laughter can be comforting and defy fear.
9. Celebrate the good times, know what's special, and claim your authority.
10. To mourn is to remember the love—comfort is always valued.

PSYCHOLOGICAL FIRST-AID CHECKLIST

This is a checklist to use to help anyone who has experienced a trauma.

1. Help people meet basic needs for food and shelter, and obtain emergency medical attention (Safety)
2. Provide repeated, simple, and accurate information on how to get these basic needs (Safety)
3. Listen to people who wish to share their stories and emotions, and remember that there is no right or wrong way to feel (Calm)
4. Be friendly and compassionate, even if people are being difficult (Calm)
5. Offer accurate information about the disaster or trauma, and the relief efforts underway to help survivors understand the situation (Calm)
6. Help people contact friends and loved ones (Connectedness)
7. Keep families together; keep children with parents or other close relatives whenever possible (Connectedness)

8. Give practical suggestions that steer people toward helping themselves (Self-Efficacy)
9. Engage people in meeting their own needs (Self-Efficacy)
10. Find out the types and locations of government and nongovernment services and direct people to those services that are available (Help)
11. When they express fear or worry, remind people (if you know) that more help and services are on the way (Help)

Source: SAMHSA, "Psychological First Aid for First Responders: Tips for Emergency and Disaster Response Workers," NMH05-0210.

Chapter Nine

Families and Comfort

LET FAMILIES DEFINE THEMSELVES

Some families are created by birth, and some are created by choice. There are single-parent families, unmarried but partnered families, and single people whose family are not blood relatives. For gay and lesbian men and women, families are often composed by choice and not by birth. Even with gay marriage, there are still parts of the country that it may not be fully accepted. After a catastrophic disaster, those seeking support may reach out for nonblood relatives. That may not coincide with a legal definition of family, but whenever possible, chosen family bonds should be respected. The success of an emotional and spiritual care operation may depend on it. Without family—however you define it—there will be no comfort.

After the crash of TWA flight 800 in 1996, I decided to sign up for the Red Cross training for their spiritual care aviation incident response team. I wanted to make sure there was at least one out gay chaplain available to provide emotional and spiritual support to gay families and other passengers of airplane crashes. I was heartened to find that the National Transportation Safety Board (NTSB) has a very inclusive definition of family and allows those profoundly grieving to determine their own family composition. During my time working with AIDS patients, however, I had seen how the legal next of kin would sometimes swoop in to claim assets after a death, even if in life they had been estranged.

After 9/11, I learned about one couple, Brad and Bruce Burlingame and their two-year-old daughter, Bella, who all died on United flight 157. I can't imagine what it would be like to not be able to use the financial and other resources that are available to straight couples and not gay couples after a disaster. Many times after mass fatality events, there are huge public fundraising efforts: for example, BostonStrong and OrlandoStrong. I remember one accountant arguing for less money for a gay man "because he probably had AIDS and wouldn't live as long as a straight husband and father and so his family was worth a much smaller monetary award." Even with the advent of gay marriage, there is still a need to be vigilant.

Any challenge the family is facing before a disaster will still be there after a disaster. If a family is having domestic violence issues before a disaster, they may be exacerbated during and after the disaster. If there is a divorce pending before a disaster, there will still be a custody agreement to work out after the disaster.

But not all changes are negative—in one shelter in Texas, disaster evacuees asked to be wed after spending days on a rooftop together during the high water. They wanted to sanctify their commitment to one another after this near-death experience.

CHILDREN AND DISASTER

Psychological first aid is part of a Red Cross training program for all volunteers that was developed after 9/11. It is based upon the concept that disaster trauma unaddressed or underaddressed leads to greater traumatic distress. I was part of the interdisciplinary committee that wrote the psychological first-aid curriculum for the Red Cross, and I was the only spiritual care professional on the team. In the first draft, the spiritual life of children was neglected until an "aha" moment when we discovered the omission. I advocated for the inclusion of children into the first psychological first-aid curriculum because children do have spiritual lives and are clearly impacted by disasters.

When dealing with a disaster, children develop resilience through the modeling of their parents or guardians. They deal with adversity with a sense of justice and fairness based upon their early formative learning. In pediatrics, the family unit is paramount in treating the child.

On September 11, elementary students witnessed the "jumpers" from the World Trade Center. Some were still walking to school with a parent or guardian when the attacks occurred.

P.S. 234 on Chambers Street was in the shadows of the towers with an outdoor playground. Some parents were in shock but still wanted to protect their children from the horrendous events occurring before their eyes. Children were exposed to repeated violent images of the planes striking the World Trade Center, the Pentagon, and the field outside Shanksville, Pennsylvania. Sometimes it's better to simply turn off the TV.

For Hurricane Katrina, it is very difficult to get the images and stories of the children out of one's memory. I particularly remember the image of a little boy who appealed for help outside the convention center. "Don't they care about us?" he asked, looking straight into news cameras. His poignant and urgent plea was unforgettable.

During the Amish school shooting in Pennsylvania, ten little girls were shot execution style, with five dying from the gunshots. The deeply religious community sought solace among their own members and forgave the shooter. The school was promptly demolished and a new one built in a distant pasture. The church family, deeply insular, and isolated by choice from much of the modern world, drew upon its religious and spiritual resources to heal and reconcile with the horrific incident. There was forgiveness for the emotional health of the family and the spiritual health of the community. Outside help was strongly discouraged and gracefully unwelcomed.

The Amish school; the elementary school in Newtown, Connecticut; the youth camp in Utoya, Norway; Parkland, Florida; and other school, church, and college shootings can seem more painful because the victims were young and innocent. They were not given the chance for full and productive lives. The perpetrator of all these crimes was a lone, male shooter.

These events strike terror in the larger public arena because they are soft targets, some appear random, others meticulously planned, and occur so quickly that help often comes too late. The Norwegian shooter of sixty-nine children at a summer camp claimed that he was sane and competent when he carried out the youth camp massacre and government bombing. He sought to end immigration and keep Norway "blond." At his trial, he fought his lawyers in their attempt to label him criminally insane and therefore not responsible for his actions. The trial found him not criminally insane. Norway does not have a death penalty and he received a prison sentence of twenty-one years, which can be extended.

Children watching news reports need to be reassured by their parents, guardians, or loved ones that they are safe with them and that a mentally ill person had committed these crimes. Age-appropriate discussions need to be held with the children of disaster and those who witness these events on television or social media. Just as children have spiritual lives, they also have an elemental sense of justice and fairness and need to be spoken to with honesty and care.

Limiting the exposure to the coverage of horrific events is the preferred approach. "A bad man did a bad thing" may be all that is comprehensible today. More explanation or a therapeutic intervention may be necessary tomorrow. Children always need to be considered as a special population with their own maturity and emotional and spiritual needs.

CHILDREN AND UTOYA: A CASE STUDY

Utoya is a disaster counselor's worst nightmare. Utoya is the small island where 69 Norwegian children were murdered on July 22, 2011, at a youth camp in Norway. I visited Utoya in 2013, two years after the killings. It was such a beautiful place and there were still shrines set up commemorating the deaths. I paid my respects and reflected on those who were killed; I gave thanks for their lives.

Utoya was about extremism and domestic terrorism. Utoya was about the "slaughter of innocents" and madness. Utoya was about remembrance and unending grief, about a parent's worst nightmare coming true, and the capacity to kill in great numbers in the safest and most remote place on the globe.

Utoya was not the beginning chapter of a history of violence in inflicting the greatest wound on the weakest victims. It was but one large paragraph of an atrocity so unfathomable it paralyzes and numbs.

Utoya was a violation of humanitarian principles and moral ethics. Utoya is now a painful fact. It's imperative to understand for those who seek to prevent "a next one" and for those who seek to prepare for the surety of a "next one."

Now, Utoya is about disaster spiritual care and not compounding an injury that may never heal by protecting the survivors and all those who knew them and loved them. It is about the information and reassurance that will be impossible to absorb and manage, and yet be crucial to knowing, and the option of knowing. How did my love one die? Where did my love one die? Who were they with or near? How long did they suffer? Where did the bullet(s) enter?

Utoya is about accountability and responsibility. Was there an emergency response plan? Was there security or protection even for the extremely remote possibility that something could happen?

Yes, the children were searched for drugs and weapons before boarding the ferry that carried them across the 1,600 feet of water that separated the island from the mainland.

Was it a reasonable "failure of the imagination" that the teenage children and their chaperones would be safe at a political party summer camp in a natural paradise?

How do you answer questions that may never have an acceptable answer?

Some considerations can be made to assist those who respond to critical events as they seek to care for those with profound, instant, unimaginable wounds:

1. Be prepared wherever you are. Knowledge lessens anxiety. Have a disaster plan and teach and practice the plan. Do not be afraid and do not be stupid. Know that these horrible events inspire more horrible events. The person convicted of the Utoya mass murder was able to assemble the bomb used as a distraction with the same information online that the Oklahoma City federal building, London Underground, and Madrid train bombers used. Fact.

2. Whether claimed as an act of war or criminal event, first things first: search and rescue before rescue and recovery. Make an assessment as best as one can. Is the location of the event safe—both for casualties and responders? Anticipate a secondary event to wound those who respond.

3. Terror may not be "random." Orchestrated for maximum physical, psychological, and spiritual pain, disasters happen and combined with wars—declared or undeclared—injuries are physical, emotional, and spiritual wounds.

4. The physical wounds may respond to treatment and heal, but the emotional and spiritual injuries may never completely heal. Does anyone ever get over the loss of a loved one? Evidence points to "it gets better" and "some days are better than others,"

but the memory remains. Some self-medicate, some sink into depression, while some seek revenge and some offer help to others who are injured in future events—well intentioned but sometimes inappropriate and sometimes with some success.

5. Has it really been over twenty years since the bombing of the Oklahoma City federal building? Nineteen years since 9/11? Twelve years since Blacksburg? Since the Newtown kindergarten murderer was inspired by the Norwegian murderer? And now Charleston, Parkland, Pittsburgh, and El Paso?

6. It is important to remember those who died. Ask their families and loved ones first what they would like to have or plan. Do not exclude those who have lost the most. Do not use numbers of fatalities. Use their names. Those who were murdered, even those who were children, had lives that mattered and those who loved them unconditionally. People who loved them into being and nurtured them and now live with unimaginable loss. Exclude family members at your peril. Even in death, respect and dignity are paramount. The dead must be buried. Their lives cut short celebrated. Rituals that deeply resonate as authentic developed and embraced.

7. Be prepared for the second wave of response in these mass fatality disasters. Those that tell the story of what happened as well as those who manipulate the story to their own selfish and political ends. Healing and return to the new normal can be delayed and distracted by those, both genuine and opportunistic.

8. Utoya was about wiping out immigration and keeping Norway blond, about killing the children of minorities and refugees. Crimes of convenience that exploit hospitality and welcome, attacks on sacred sanctuaries where children can play, and adults can be inspired, and futures can be hopeful.

9. People are always afraid of those who are different. The key is to educate ourselves and learn to embrace differences.

I think a lot about Utoya, as the headlines report about El Paso. Very different disasters, very different criminal acts, so convenient in an open society, where one has so much opportunity to harm and far less urgency to do good. Some are houses of worship and also houses of hospitality, and much like Utoya, they are now seemingly targets.

And these words from the father of one of the Parkland students seem fitting to end here. "If you had known my child, you would not have killed him."

THE ELDERLY

After Katrina, one elderly New Orleans congregation bought their own buses for evacuation (and Sunday school), because trust with government had been broken for a timely and safe prelandfall evacuation for future storms. Then the British Petroleum oil rig exploded and millions of tons of oil leaked into the Gulf. Suddenly, the congregation started to plan for an "oil-i-cane" with wind-driven oil being carried on land, and into inhabited communities, dealing possibly with wind damage and everything exposed, being covered in crude oil or sitting in toxic water.

Nursing home residents sitting in water up to their chests and their telephone calls for help are some of the most haunting images coming out of Hurricane Harvey in Texas. The world witnessed the powerlessness of the nursing home residents and the first responders to get to them for rescue and evacuation. Prisons were evacuated more swiftly than some advanced care facilities. Did the nursing homes have a disaster plan? Hopefully. Perhaps they relied upon local government and owners to provide transport and materials. In some glaring instances, the elderly residents were temporarily abandoned.

A nursing home fire in Arkansas left more than a hundred residents without their medications, hearing aids, and glasses. The elderly may find it difficult to put together a "go" bag with medications, important papers, and so forth in case of an emergency. In this case, a family health colleague was able to secure help from a national pharmaceutical organization and local opticians supplied the elderly residents with glasses.

I have already mentioned the well-meaning Jewish nursing home attendant who, during Hurricane Katrina's evacuation, wrote the number of medical record files on the arms of those being evacuated from New Orleans to Houston. I've also talked about the bus that caught fire with elderly residents being evacuated from Houston to Dallas during Hurricane Rita. The fire was exacerbated by the number of elderly with oxygen tanks on the bus. Medically frail individuals have significant needs during and after a disaster.

MILITARY FAMILIES

Disasters share much in common with battlefields. The walking wounded, emotionally damaged, PTSD, secondary PTSD—all can be found postdisaster in the affected community. The closer to the disaster event, the more physical, emotional, and spiritual damage can be anticipated. Military families on active duty face the tremendous stress of daily life while a spouse is in a combat theater. There were numerous reports of active duty soldiers in Iraq unable to assist their families facing the devastation after hurricanes and watching helplessly as their colleagues in the National Guard were called in for domestic disaster assistance.

While adapting psychological first aid to military families, the project title and focus became, "Coping with Deployment." Our nation has been in a state of war since just after September 11—nineteen-plus years—and during that time there have been multiple mass fatality natural and human-caused disasters including the shooting at Ft. Hood, Texas, and the Navy Yard in Washington, DC, in 2013.

The modern battlefield gives our warriors cellphones and laptops and extreme connectedness with families and loved ones at home. However, separation stress during crisis at home—miscarriages, death in the family, and financial matters—kept the Red Cross crisis line switchboard busy with operators receiving suicide threats and other critical messages.

PETS

When we let people define the composition of their own families, that definition may include a dog or cat. One of the lessons learned from recent disasters, but primarily since Hurricane Katrina, was that some people will not evacuate without their pets, even on peril of death or injury. Before Katrina, most shelters were "people only" and did not have space or sanitation/safety requirements for domestic animals. There were heartbreaking photographs of abandoned dogs on rooftops with others chained to porches. For some, the elderly or those who live alone, their dog or cat may have been their only remaining "family" member. Faced with the dilemma of abandoning an elderly person who will not leave their dog, or simply taking the dog along, many advocated for cosheltering. Animal organizations began setting up next to human shelters. This turned out to be a win-win for everyone.

While working at the Red Cross, I decided to attend the first "Animals in Disaster" conference in Sacramento in 2008. At this meeting, many state and local animal control and welfare agencies came together to emphasize the need to include pet and livestock evacuations in disaster evacuation and sheltering plans. There was even an animal first-aid course offered where we learned "mouth to snout" resuscitation! After ten years working in disaster spiritual care management, and another eight years in hospital and hospice settings as a chaplain, I need and receive much emotional and spiritual support from my own dogs. I was glad to learn more about how to care for them in case of a disaster.

Years after the September 11 attacks, years into the Iraq invasion and continuing battles in Afghanistan, the renewed emotional and spiritual support value of trained canine units is well documented. At home, many groups have matched dogs with returning combat veterans, and the expansion of pet therapies for emotional and spiritual support services has grown across healthcare.

Military chaplains, healthcare chaplains, and disaster chaplains can advocate for the inclusion of companion animals, as well as the family dog, as part of the reentry into civilian life or as support for the chronically ill patient. When disaster strikes, a community response plan should also include a provision for the evacuation, care, and feeding of the entire household—which may include a dog, cat, parrot, or pony.

For those who are taking care of our soldiers abroad and public safety officers at home, improving the end-of-life care of their patients, or being the compassionate presence after the storm or flood, self-care is basic and nonnegotiable. For some, that care may come from the family dog. From rural America to studio apartments in the city, dogs serve as companions for children, the elderly, and all types of families, and work as guardians, sentries, protectors, and "cures" for isolation and depression.

Battlefront dogs have companioned and served our nation by supporting our troops—individuals and units—as morale boosters, humanitarian search and rescue, bomb snifters, and scouts. Stateside reunions may appear extravagant unless one has had their life saved by a unit canine. There are memorial monuments to heroic canine "soldiers," and the services of animals in war, on Park Lane in London and in South Africa, and for humanitarian service in Central Park. The emotional and spiritual impact, the cultural interpretation and power of the story have intense value. The emotional and spiritual impact of the theatrical version of *War Horse*, about a young man's thoroughbred drafted into World War I battle, has been mentioned and fully documented. Baby boomers, who grew up with Lassie, Old Yeller, and Rin Tin Tin also had Noah's Ark and the Good Shepard. The traumatized and vulnerable may remember hope, may identify care, and transcend momentary pain and suffering when reunited with a canine best friend.

A society may be judged on how it cares for the most vulnerable, special populations including children, the elderly, those with functional needs, and animals. In natural disasters and human-caused disasters, i.e., the accidental and the criminal, our environment (and impact) is shared.

For myself, I treat my own compassion fatigue through, in part, the animal kingdom: our family dogs, the backyard birds, and the giraffes and pandas that live three miles away in the zoo. I was called in to the National Zoo when a red panda cub died. I offered my services as a grief/crisis counselor for caretaker/animal keeper staff. There has been much anticipation and anxiety about the seventy-year-old female elephant, Ambika, dying because she has been at the zoo so long and has such a deep relationship with her keepers and the public.

New training for capturing and caring for animals in disaster, such as emergency evacuation plans for horses and other livestock, now exist and are normal considerations for the extreme abnormal event— the flood, earthquake, or wildfire. There practices are not only humane, but also good business and government practice.

A two-week-old baby pulled from the rubble lifts the emotions and spirits of earthquake rescuers amidst great destruction, death, and despair. Though certainly not the equivalent to a successful human rescue, many also celebrate the retrieval of a puppy from a collapsed apartment block. When hope has been dimmed, any sign of life may give considerable solace and peace and add meaning and comfort to those who risk their lives to save others, and the greater world that supports their efforts.

Thirty-eight years into the AIDS pandemic, in reflection and remembrance, I am grateful for pets in hospice settings—a smaller historical coda to a time when "failure to thrive" was part of an end-of-life diagnosis. Yes, this hospice chaplain walked dogs.

With hospice, the need to include domestic pets into the treatment plan for the emotional health and spiritual support of the chronically ill patient is well documented. Dogs and cats were welcome and could spend the night in the patients' beds and give solace and comfort, and, for some, unconditional love. Oftentimes, that was their dog, loyal to the end.

I remember my patients. I remember my colleagues and team. I remember their families. I remember what helped sustain some and comfort others when disowned by family and religion.

WHAT ABOUT THE PERPETRATOR'S FAMILY/COMMUNITY?

After a tragedy, the perpetrator's family and community is also in need of comfort and support. It's not fair to blame the whole Muslim community for the actions of one extremist, and so the weekend after the Pulse shooting, I visited two mosques in greater Orlando. I prayed with the men and boys and was given a chair though I do not consider myself elderly or disabled. I prayed silently in gratitude for the opportunity to be there, be unafraid, and express support for the Islamic community that was blamed for killing forty-nine. One of the mosques I referred to as the yuppie mosque because many young professionals attended. I broke the fast at both mosques and shared in a spicy feast.

One young boy in a polo shirt gave me a name tag reading, "Ambassador of Islam." He was so appreciative when I put it on and wore it. My female spiritual and mental health care colleagues showed solidarity with the women and girls and even spoke, breaking protocol for visitors, but empowered by the level of fear perceived at the service. *Stop the Hate* T-shirts were purchased as a young person's fundraiser, and this important outreach was successful, at least for one night, with community guests providing symbolic and physical support for the Islamic centers. The way we treat those who are most vulnerable in society is an indication of how healthy a society is, not just as a matter of justice, it's also a matter of mercy. Comforting is showing mercy.

THERE HAS BEEN A DEATH IN THE FAMILY

As comforters, our ability and capacity to be empathic is vital in providing emotional and spiritual support even when there is a death in the family. This is being written after the latest school shooting.

"I'M A GOOD PERSON, SO WHY WAS I SHOT?"

What does it mean to really survive? What was it like before mass shootings were routine? These questions from the morning newspaper resonated and triggered these thoughts.

Mass shootings are the price America pays for ignoring gun safety. Normal people can buy guns. Crazy people can buy guns. Battle enactors can buy guns. Criminals can buy guns. Children have access to guns. Most Americans now have access to guns to defend their skyscrapers and condos, timeshares and cabins, from Native Americans and oppressors. No one can enslave us. No one can take over our country because we have guns in every home in America, and we are much safer as a nation. Except when we have random anticipated mass shootings. Random anticipated memorial services and presidential visits. Random anticipated mass shootings and classroom slaughter. Nightclub shootings as gunfire punctuates percussion.

Municipalities that have contracted for temporary morgue services in advance of anticipated mass fatality incidences. Response plans that assume someone is going to kill a lot of people somewhere nearby in the near future. Where chaos is a normal budget consideration and an assured expectation. Not if, but when.

Because of our humanity, for some, because of their faith, because of our sense of basic justice, and our hope that someone will be there to help us in a critical future incident, we buy guns. We also train for the first few minutes, the first hour, what to do when we know what will happen. The response and the rescue. The heroic and the critical, the automatic neutralization of the perpetrator.

The good guy kills the bad guy.

We train for crisis. We train for consequences.

When does a history of violence become a collection of memorials and annual gatherings? Almost every day.

Almost every day is the anniversary of a mass shooting. Almost every day people gather to remember a loved one killed in an act of mass violence. Almost every day someone reads a name that has been shortened to a number. Almost every day we recall a husband or father, son or daughter, who died in a flurry of gunfire or shot at close range in the back of their head.

We imagine what they could have been, what they might have done, what celebrations they could have planned and attended, what comfort and love they could have shared with us if only they hadn't been shot.

Guns do kill people. And guns are never around when you need them to stop a mass shooting until it's too late.

If we ignored mass shootings, didn't give them any publicity, would they go away? How much of this is seeking immortality through infamy? Knowing that in one's last breath, the headline with one's name is already created with identification the only minute delay in broadcasting it to the world. I wonder who will be killed today.

Will I be shot today?

My great, great grandfather was a minuteman. There was a Revolutionary War. I am from a long line of veterans.

My right to own and carry a gun is guaranteed by the Second Amendment. Does my right to clean water, a decent job and home, the right to an education and equal justice under the law have any less importance?

How about police and other law enforcement only having the option of carrying a gun? An imperfect solution to mass shootings? Or do we write off mass shootings as collateral damage and the price of freedom in modern society?

Yes, there are bad cops. Yes, the idea is realized already, but the assumption of surrendering instruments of war not peace keeping domestically—should be tried. Do mass shootings need to continue, to be routine?

Mass shootings are not routine for those who respond to them. Police and EMTs may be military veterans. One survived Afghanistan and Iraq, but what about Orlando? What toll accumulates with every tragic incident? Are they still tragedies if we know they are going to happen?

Not only what does it mean to lose someone we know and love in a routine mass shooting, the question is this: What does it mean to survive?

Yes, you are alive, perhaps with a gunshot wound, nicely healing, but what does that mean?

You will need emotional and, for some, spiritual support. The first question always is "Why did it happen to me?" The question "Is the gunman finished?" will be followed by "Will there be another round of gunfire? Did my friends survive? What was the extent of their injuries? Will we be able to dance again? Make love like we did before the gunshots? Will I ever be comfortable again?"

Who will help me go to the bathroom? Who will pay my rent? Who will drive me to rehab or future doctor appointments?

Who will hold me in the night when I have nightmares or feel guilty that I lived when so many others died? Who will take care of me? Or, I'm overwhelmed with emotions and pain and can't go on? Or, let me join my friends in death because we'll be together again and be able to dance in heaven.

To dance in heaven. We are all angel sparkle butter and the glitter so much better framed by rainbows and sunbeams. Yes, "We are stardust, we are golden" and "We've got to get ourselves back to the garden." These dreams give me comfort.

Why is it normal to see more suicides in places where there have been mass shootings? Why does the gunfire never really end after the gun smoke evaporates?

Bullets are psychological as well as in cartridges. Everyone knows that. That is only stating the obvious until it happens to you or someone you know, you love. There is a sting before one really knows what is happening, then a crack, a sound, and quickly the realization that this is finally happening to me. Now is the time that I need help. Perhaps there is someone around me that I can still help. I need to stop the bleeding.

I think there has to be a better way. I think we can enact some reasonable restrictions, while still upholding the spirit of the Second Amendment. It will be hard, it will involve hard conversations, but believe me—it's easier than burying the victim of another shooting. It's easier than explaining to another mother why she won't be able to see her son grow up. It's easier than telling another wife that her husband will never come home.

WAYS TO COMFORT

1. Say thank you to a policeman or fireman today.
2. Help a senior put together a "go" bag.
3. Always have a flashlight.
4. Express gratitude to helpers in the community.
5. Clarify and illuminate hope.
6. If it was wrong before the disaster, it is wrong during and after the disaster.
7. Children are not invisible and are impacted by disasters and need comfort.
8. Do not impose your cultural norms on others with different cultural norms.

9. Talk to children honestly, but age appropriately.
10. Ask about someone's family with care and no judgment.

Chapter Ten

The Future of Comfort

We comfort because we care. We comfort because we love. We comfort because of the Golden Rule. A late colleague at the National Transportation Safety Board said it best: "If something happens to me, who will walk my mother through the airport to get to where I am?"

We are the sum of our experiences —our knowledge and our training—that allow and require us to comfort. I couldn't have been one of the founders of disaster spiritual care at the Red Cross if I hadn't lived through the AIDS epidemic in New York City. If I hadn't been exposed to princesses and poverty, how could I relate to those whose life resources and perspective are so dramatically different yet contain the same need for support following trauma? If I hadn't worked at the Cabrini Hospice and personally lost all those friends, how could I sit with those who had just lost their loved one in a plane crash or hurricane? If I hadn't seen the beauty of whales in Antarctica and leopards in South Africa, the birds of Brazil, and koalas in Australia, how could I sit with the violence of the natural world after disasters like Katrina and Harvey? If I hadn't appreciated and valued the extraordinary gifts and opportunities that I have been given, how could I sit and companion those who have lost everything?

Finding and offering comfort starts in the good times during the joy and celebration of living in relationships and light and love. Creating memories and cherishing them. Trauma accumulates and throws life terribly out of balance. Catastrophes are violent and unjust. Disasters take and destroy and erase.

137

Responding to disasters is not for everybody. There are those who may be enduring illness, or recent death, and need to mourn fully and honestly. It's okay to say, "No, now is not a good time." Sometimes I feel that I have spent ten years at Ground Zero and that one more death will push me over the edge; that in my woundedness I can't tolerate one more death. There are times when, even with intense clinical training, small group process and support, disciplined self-care and expertise, death becomes intolerable. Any death.

But I keep going. I keep going in memory of my colleagues like Marcia and Susan and so many unnamed but not forgotten partners in relief. I keep going because of victims like the young boy who begged for help after Katrina. I keep going for all those who were senselessly cut down in Orlando. It is a cliché, but death truly doesn't take a holiday, and it is both my honor and my duty to keep going.

There are those whose gifts for advocacy and social justice define a speaking role for those who have lost everything. And there are those who seek mercy and meaning in the catastrophic nature of things and the violence that continue to plague us every day. I have learned not to put a Band-Aid on a broken bone or a cold compress on a broken heart. All disaster victims and survivors should have equal access to emergency assistance and long-term care. I have an inherent sensitivity to marginalized people, and I have found that instances of discrimination can be very subtle in disaster.

Finding comfort is about our need to help other people. Finding comfort is about helping ourselves by helping other people. As Anton Boisen, a famous American chaplain, once said, "It's about being deeply enough connected with ourselves and the Ground of Being that we are able to accurately take in the available information and use it with wisdom for the well-being of others and self."

Even with profound faith, group nurture, prayer, and the support of a wise and seasoned team, part of our humanity is the realization that no one is immune to the horrors and complexities of death. It's not normal to wish to die or to work with death, to chaplain those traumatized by the killing fields of war, planes that fall out of the sky, mall and movie theater and school shootings, or the increasing strength and duration of Big Killer Weather.

Working in disaster has made me see the need for more public services, more public health, public safety, public education, and better housing. There are so many unmet needs and so many persons who need our help. A chaplain can apply a tourniquet but also needs to know when it's time to step back and allow others to take over.

THE POWER OF CELEBRITY

The American Red Cross has a celebrity cabinet that would raise money and morale for the organization. After major catastrophic disasters there would be a telethon that would raise millions of dollars. The power of celebrity to comfort, to fund raise, to publicize disasters is phenomenal. Think of Brad Pitt and Harry Connick Jr. after Hurricane Katrina. Remember Bruce Springsteen singing in Madison Square Garden after 9/11. And all the country music stars that pulled together after the massive shooting in Las Vegas. These are the ways that celebrity focuses the attention of the public not only on the victims but on the need for continuing aid.

DISASTER COMES TO EVERYONE

Disaster comes to everyone. Disaster comes to the comforter. While I was modeling in Milan in 1989, I received word that my father had had a stroke in Columbia, Missouri. I immediately flew home to say goodbye. Unfortunately, he passed before I could get there. While he lay dying, I had been sitting on a British Airways 747 that was delayed because of a fire in the airport kitchen. When I finally arrived home, I was comforted by my mother, sister, aunts, nieces, nephews, and cousins. The only clergy present, besides me, was my cousin John.

I was wearing sunglasses, but one could tell that I was crying. Everyone knew that I had been on assignment in Milan, but as was pointed out by one cousin, it was my appearance modeling a windbreaker in the JC Penney catalog that cemented my celebrity, even with a small *c*.

At the funeral, we played my father's favorite Count Basie tune, while my sister and I spoke celebrating his life. My dad was finally at peace, while I was full of grief and pain. This personal tragedy only inspired me to have more compassion when helping others whose pain is so much more public.

Disasters changed me. Wherever there is suffering, there is a need for comfort. There is a need for much information and reassurance. Yet there may also be anger for the seeming randomness of whatever has occurred. Often I found myself repeating the following prayer of lamentation silently.

> Let me tell you how I am helping. Let me tell you how much I care. Let me not blame you for living in harm's way. Let me not blame you for being poor. Let me not preach caution and vigilance. Help me understand how the water got in your screen doors. I'm sorry for your losses and living on the Gulf Coast. I'm standing in the middle of the highway and wiping the camera lens so staging can be visible to the nation and the world. I am here to bear witness. I'm here to tell the story of your suffering to comfort those in another world. I know bad things happen to good people. I know that umbrellas float away. I want so much to save you, to save anybody, I want my life to matter. I want to comfort and grieve for the world before the flood. I want to see photographs from before the rain. I want the buses to arrive. I want basic emergency needs. I want people to know how much pain there is underwater. I need to trust and obey. Amen.

Victims of these disaster will be forever changed and, for some, forever defined by the plane crash, the tornado in the night, the explosion, and the gunshot.

One knows that if you are in close proximity to a natural or human-caused disaster, you already are a first responder by being in the wrong place at the right time (or right place at the wrong time). One is also a victim and basically needs to get out of harm's way. You can help with immediate needs (e.g., getting the kids out of the school bus), but then you become a liability in due order and get in the way of those specially trained in search and rescue or search and recovery. During the Minneapolis bridge collapse, for example, well-meaning drivers in cars already pulled over to safety were eager to help rescue the school children on the teetering bus. However, by the time emergency personnel arrived, they were more of a hindrance than a help as their lack of training impeded the safety of all concerned.

I admire and honor many police and fire chaplains and military chaplains I've met in my four decades doing this work. They are a profession of comforters. I've had the privilege to present at their national conferences and work as a member of training and planning teams who advocated for a common operational field, an infrastructure of partners making immediate sense of the destruction, and pinpointing where the competition to care is addressed and best practices established.

One of the most valuable principles is this: the closer one may be assigned to disaster victims and their loved ones, the higher the professional credentials needed. And those credentials are based upon experience and training, and skills gained from presence and use in disaster settings whether it is in the emergency room or flood plain, a burning nightclub or bloodied classroom.

Yet I have realized that there may be no such thing as a perfect response. Disasters change everyone, victim and volunteer alike. When one returns home one both celebrates helping those in need and mourns for the devastation encountered. It may take years to accept the new reality, the new normal. It may take years for wounds to be mended and healed. This is true for both responders and victims.

When Hurricane Katrina devastated the Gulf Coast, the entire nation and globe witnessed our domestic horror with thousands dead and separated, assistance under-equipped and under-staffed, spontaneous and delayed, and the unprecedented response of humanitarian assistance from around the globe. Hurricanes Harvey and Maria revealed our powerlessness. The story is still being written including our part, the chaplaincy part, the faith community response, the health and mental healthcare part.

The chaos and destruction after disasters of any kind helped me see the value and importance of a strong group of first responders and community emergency manager leaders. Disaster devastation helped me see the importance of a strong and robust public safety initiative that incorporates gun safety and strong mental health initiatives. Working in disaster helped me understand that in the absence of effective schools, hospitals, and other community institutions, a community takes much longer to heal. And finally, insuring that families have good, safe schools and housing before a disaster means their recovery will be much quicker after.

If we commit to furthering public service, health, safety, and education, we will be so much better prepared when disasters occur. I suggest the following initiatives to strengthen communities and help them recover after disaster occurs.

1. Public service. Recommit ourselves to the honor and privilege of public service. Understanding the strong ethical requirements of public service that is its primary mission as well as its job. Your personal benefit is not economic; it is the awareness that your efforts have made your community a better place by helping our

communities become more livable and our families' future brighter.

2. Public safety. We commit ourselves to an ultimate type of public service by keeping our communities safe. Our schools safe. Our homes and futures free from fear. Police and fire personnel are generally the most visible representatives for public safety, yet we live in a nation where the public trust in law enforcement has suffered greatly. How can we be safe if those entrusted with our safety are on the firing line from both liberals and conservatives? Are our police officers and fire personnel safer because more people have guns? Police officers need to be supported and should be the only ones packing heat in our communities to insure the public safety. Politicizing fear and demonizing difference divide us as a nation and a family. Yes, there are bad cops, however, police must operate today on the premise that everyone is carrying a gun, even children, and it only takes a split second to kill someone, often someone of color. Standing your ground is meaningless when everyone is afraid of each other and everyone feels they need a gun to protect themselves.

3. Public health. Commit ourselves to keeping water and air safe. Keep the institutions in our community thriving and healthy. Make healthcare accessible to all, particularly the elderly and children. Develop preventative health initiatives that regulate sugar and fat as a threat to public health, safety, and our welfare along with tobacco, alcohol, and firearms. Mutually assured destruction worked until the costs of building fortresses were no longer effective deterrents. Traditional threats to the health and welfare of our community need to be reevaluated. Future public health threats are not known today. Health challenges may be global in nature and need a global response. We need safe food, food that does not debilitate or paralyze us, food for sustenance and not as the result of addiction to sugar.

4. Public education. Just as there is a human right to dignity, to be respected, and to equality, there is a human right to clean water, safe communities, and schools. The right to read and write, to speak and to lead, to serve and protect—all people need a foundation of a basic education amidst culture and tradition. Education about our history and legacy that must be cherished in a democracy and maintained. We must commit to revaluing edu-

cation to improve our lives, and not let it be devalued by those who feel an educated body politic only questions authority.

We can't prevent all disasters from occurring. They are part of life. But if we devote ourselves to these basic public commitments, all society will be improved and social justice championed and embraced. Alongside the Four Freedoms enshrined as Freedom of Worship, Freedom from Want, Freedom from Fear, and Freedom of Speech, this is my blueprint for hope. This is what I hope continues to be called "America." And hope is sacred. In a disaster, a strong community with strong institutions and leaders will hasten recovery, even in the worst possible scenario, and that will comfort all of us.

THE NEW DARK AGES

The kids will be extremely angry that their cellphones and iPads don't work. They may think grandma's house is a museum of old things like a landline phone that they don't know how to work. One may not remember log-ins on a new computer and be unable to access one's account. The car's battery dies because there is no place to charge it, or older models run out of gas.

The challenges of preparedness will be extremely daunting and parents will need to work diligently with their children or those who are in their care to memorize a disaster plan. There will be a need to memorize telephone numbers and log-ins in the new dark ages. There will be a need to practice dialing on a landline and knowing what numbers to "dial." Family life must not stop if the cellphones don't work. There has to be a back-up plan.

Do you know addresses of close relatives one may ask children and practice repeating key information like telephone numbers and concrete locations? Do you know someone with a landline if a family member doesn't have one? Small children may be mystified and a bit confused by having to push all the numbers on a landline and, for some phones, "Talk."

And, finally, always have a back-up plan.

I personally can't imagine what it's like to have a school-age child today or be the parent of a school-age child. These children have been practicing active shooter drills since kindergarten and have developed resilience beyond comprehension. They just do it and experience it as another "game" in an average school day.

In the future, school children may have go bags in their cubbies in case they have to shelter in place overnight. Being a teacher today has far more responsibilities and concerns that are shared by parents.

Public transportation may be shut down as occurred on September 11 in Washington, DC, and New York City.

There will need to be more creative ways of comforting with an entirely new batch of considerations.

And what about those who are suffering from health and mental health issues before the catastrophic event? A colleague has a friend who is terrified of mall shootings and is unable to go to a shopping center or even a school. This friend has never been in close proximity to one of these events but has been sickened by repeated news of the latest shootings in a mall, movie theater, synagogue, or school. How many others share the same anxiety and fear and what are the mental health costs and solutions to help these people who are legitimately suffering. This is something that can't be solved with a "mall chaplain" but may need the help of a licensed mental health counselor to be comforted and treated.

There are vast numbers of people who suffer from mental illness and already think that the world has gone crazy, and then one adds a mass fatality event.

It is not fear mongering to know how to do CPR or apply a tourniquet. It will be a comfort knowing basic first aid.

How does one deal with money if credit cards don't work? One may still be able to text a donation to the Red Cross, but what about rumors of a food riot? This may not be far-fetched due to the number of looting incidents after major disasters. Civil unrest and disorder may become the norm and not the exception. There will be tremendous needs for comfort and reassurance if one cannot feed their family or heat one's home.

There are many agencies working to ensure that this "Brave New World" will never exist, but our increasing dependency on technology for extremely basic things like communication and sustenance is real.

What about the impact of yearly floods, and weekly shootings? What about when the nation moves on to the newer disaster, without adequately comforting those with longer-term care needs like rebuilding homes and lives? Who will drive one to long-term rehabilitation centers for physical and mental therapy? Who will help pay the bills?

Will there be comforters, someone to talk to, when people's attention moves on to newer catastrophes?

What about the future of chaplaincy? Of emotional and spiritual care providers and comforters when scarce resources may eliminate support for an entire new generation of comforters? There will always be a need for comforters as long as there are traumatic events.

Technology has changed the entire way one conducts business and how one reacts to disaster. Texting and GoFundMe campaigns have raised millions of dollars for the American Red Cross and individuals. There may be an entire generation that doesn't know what checks are. When our home was broken into, credit cards were stolen but the checkbook was not. When facing a personal challenge like recovering from a disaster or health issue, how will people cope? Will there be enough comforters that know how to provide emotional and spiritual support beyond material needs?

When I started at the American Red Cross, there were designated family and friends reception sites where parents and other loved ones could reconnect with their children or spouses in the event of a mass fatality disaster. Today, children are able to text their parents where they are, to call them from inside the classroom under attack, to call from the ambulance to say, if they are able, which hospital they are being taken to, and from the emergency room all in real time.

Few have time to read the newspaper a day later about a disaster event when they can get immediate updates on Twitter or Facebook. There will be those who read newspapers online that are frequently updated, but news is much more immediate, information is much more immediate, and people are traumatized by media exposure of events occurring halfway around the globe. Shootings in Nairobi have the impact of shootings in Pittsburgh for some. There is a profound need for comfort, and much of it comes electronically from social media communities online.

There is a theory that social media devices decrease empathy and isolates people more in today's society. That will impact those who are trying to provide comfort but are unsure as to who needs comfort because one is not in a community setting but may be home alone. Some disasters are more complicated than 140 characters.

There is also a hopeful trend to not publicize the assailant and make him infamous. That is a first step that should be reaffirmed and to keep the focus on the victims and survivors—those who are in great need of comfort. That's what occurred in New Zealand after the Christchurch mosque shootings.

In some parts of the world, gruesome images of a catastrophe are broadcast and not censored in anyway. Television screens are red with the blood and bodies of those killed in a terrorist bombing or plane crash in the Ukraine. Should the media here become more graphic for impact and viewership? How do these images impact the healing occupations, the comforters? It makes their job much harder dealing with things that magnify trauma.

Sometimes when I'm asked about the comforting fields, I think about wildflower meadows, and it makes me think about Thoreau's idea of "forest bathing," going out in the greenery and immersing oneself in nature for its healing and therapeutic value, and without an iPhone! Could a new generation of comforters relax or would they be so anxious to have lost connectivity that one was incapable of empathy? There are major personality traits in comforters like the ability to show kindness and mercy. There are also those who advocate for social justice that show characteristics of perseverance and endurance.

There will be a great need for humanitarians who support the need for emotional and spiritual care because of their belief in the future of humanity. There will be those who learn or know how to manage comfort and see it as a sacred trust, to help one's fellow man even after repeated traumas that exposure to daily media may cause.

The next generation of spiritual care professionals will know how to comfort and also advocate for the need for comfort. There will continue to be a need for priests and prophets, individuals and communities, who know the importance of emotional and spiritual support in a highly technical world and thrive where they are.

There will be those who still value the power of prayer and the sacred nature of life. We must value and support these future healers.

My humble suggestion would be to consider taking a course in clinical pastoral education or in community emergency response training. The latter is available free of charge in some locales and the former is for those who wish to work with more traumatic disasters.

VISITORS BRIGHTEN PEOPLE'S DAYS: WHEN RELIGION AND CULTURE CONFLICTS WITH COMFORT

The tragic school shootings across the country have focused our attention on this type of disaster. This is a criminal act. "We're not supposed to lose our children in school," an administrator was quoted on the television that morning. In the classroom of the Amish school, a sign hanging on the wall provided cruel irony as ten little girls were bound and shot: "Visitors Brighten People's Days."

What if comfort from the larger community outside the Amish is not requested or needed? What does the comforter do? What if the prevailing culture does not want outside comforting? One must respect the religious beliefs and culture of others.

> The Amish are a resilient, resourceful people who address life through their deep Christian faith and lifestyles. The foundation of their faith is bolstered by their extensive sense of self-dependence within their communities. They know what is available to them and will reach out as they deem appropriate.
>
> What we consider a "disaster" is not a disaster to them. An untoward event becomes an opportunity for strengthening their already solid bonds of compassion, love and caring amongst their people. Such an event is a "happening" or "'occurrence" of common life and living. It is clearly a part of God's plan that is accepted with honor. Indeed, there is sadness, however, such an event does not cause them to react with fear for life.[1]

Comfort may need an invitation and may not always be culturally desirable or viable. Religious belief and practice may not be understood by outsiders.

THE CHALLENGES OF COMFORT AND THE DISASTER EMERGENCY OF INFECTION

Ebola is another challenge to the comforter. Ebola was and is, again, a global healthcare disaster centered in Africa, a threat to national security, and, for some, a threat to religious freedom. It has been spread due to burial practices of indigenous religious practices. Upon death, bodies are embraced and washed ceremoniously, which then transfers the Ebola virus to those preparing the body for burial. This viral transmission generally infects close family members who are doing the washing and passes along the virus, which is usually fatal. Government and health-care workers had to educate and secure areas of contamination and develop new methods of mourning and burial so that the virus was contained.

Emotional and spiritual care comfort must take place behind a mask and other personal protective equipment. Stress on medical personnel also presents challenges for comfort. Currently, the US Public Health Service and the International Red Cross and Red Crescent Society are monitoring and involved in the outbreak. The Ebola outbreak is also taking place in an armed conflict zone that impedes halting the virus and magnifying the emergency.

Taking care of the sick and less fortunate is a tenet of all major global religions. Faith groups originally founded our hospitals as part of their mission. Texas Presbyterian Hospital is where the first person in America with Ebola died. It is also the same hospital where the first American became infected in the last outbreak in 2014.

The infection of several American physicians and other healthcare workers was the result of a faith community mission to Africa, to help where the help is needed the most. Medical missionaries have a long tradition of service from founding hospitals and medical schools in China to Africa, whether the threat is a new or known infectious dis-ease, or response to a natural or human-caused disaster, such as the earthquake in Haiti or the AIDS pandemic. There have been many lessons learned, and one needs to remember wisdom gained from the service and sacrifice of those who have gone before us. Healthcare and comfort are part of that long tradition.

What do chaplains (spiritual care professionals) have to do with biological, viral threats? Military and healthcare chaplains have gener-ally been on the front lines in the critical care and urgent emergency medical response to these new infectious agents as well as preparing necessary emotional and spiritual support. Be not afraid, but be in-formed.

Airport healthcare screenings are nothing new. Remember SARS (severe acute respiratory syndrome)? Infections in 2004 spread across the globe due to global air travel, and culture played a part in its transmission. Passengers getting off international flights had their tem-perature taken at major hub airports in the United States and across the world. Due to many fatalities in China, and the absence of a vaccine, some passengers with fever were quarantined. After SARS was iden-tified and the public was educated about its transmission and containment, knowledge lessened anxiety. Still, there is a profound need for support and comfort.

Public health working with global media shared the advances in the identification of the virus that caused AIDS and how one could prevent the transmission through the exchange of bodily fluids, needle exchange, and the vital dialog about religious practice. Therefore, what we learned about AIDS helped us when we had the SARS outbreak in 2004.

As soon as the CDC and the World Health Organization could mobilize and identify the cause and source of the SARS virus, an action plan was made to contain and treat the virus. However, a passenger(s) who flew transcontinental transmitted the SARS virus from China and Southeast Asia to Canada.

At the same time, after the September 11 attacks on our nation, weapons of mass destruction/terrorism concerns also came to include biological and chemical weapons. All hazard plans for preparedness and response became a regular part of local emergency response and also our healthcare industry. Medical centers regularly practiced emergency response drills along with first responders from police and fire departments, which extended from national, state, and local stakeholders to including our military, now tasked with protecting the homeland. Emotional and spiritual care comforters are essential elements of the emergency response plan.

Hospital chaplains are trained regularly about PPEs (personal protective equipment) and regularly wear it when visiting the extremely vulnerable in pediatric neonatal, oncology, and other intensive care units. One must wear protective covering including masks and gowns to prevent infections to the incredibly vulnerable patient. Fear of infecting a patient as well as a patient infecting a healthcare worker or visitor created an essential standard of care and practice in these acute settings. There was still the need for comfort as families dealt with the critical health issues.

I called the pastoral care director of the Toronto hospital that cared for a majority of SARS patients during that 2002 outbreak in Canada that started in China. I asked about reflections made and best practices in the weeks after the crisis passed.

My colleague shared that the initial email request and follow-up phone call came somewhat as a surprise. When one is in the eye of the hurricane, one's focus in where it needs to be—there, in the moment and not focused on rebuilding, but on merely surviving, hour by hour, day by day.

Initially, the hospital management had made the decision to dismiss all nonessential personnel from the acute care campus; doctors and nurses would shelter in place for the treatment and care of their critically ill patients. Chaplains were among those excluded from the critical care core group until after the first day of the quarantine. What was experienced was a spike in anxiety by both healthcare workers and patients. There was no one inside the bubble to deal with the profound emotional and spiritual issues identified in those early hours. There was no one there to offer comfort and reassurance. There was no one to represent hope. Highly credentialed healthcare chaplains, who are clinically trained and board certified, know how to be the nonanxious presence whether in the healthcare arena or heat of battle. War on AIDS. War on SARS. War on Ebola. War on measles.

The chaplains in the Toronto medical center were invited back for their essential specialties; supporting and comforting the staff and supporting and comforting their patients dealing with unimaginable anxiety. But the quarantine for SARS was already broken. The cultural and religious practices of one of the nurses compelled him to attend Saturday evening worship services in his local congregation, which potentially exposed upward of another 120 persons to the virus that caused SARS. Normally, the threat of exposing others is cause enough for public health and local law enforcement to prevent a larger potential healthcare risk, but, in this instance, few could imagine this scenario. How could a healthcare professional defy the quarantine? There are those who believe that their faith will protect them from infection and transmission. However, there were Toronto congregations that cancelled worship services and developed a telephone tree to deliver meals to the elderly or homebound. Comfort was also delivered through these same methods. Imagine the fear and need for comfort? Imagine the cultural challenges and impediments to comfort.

Visitors could spread disease and traditional methods of comforting may also spread disease. Outbreaks of infectious diseases create great fear and anxiety and the need for emotional and spiritual care. The need for comfort is extremely evident.

On September 11, I was chaplain educator on staff at a Washington, DC, hospital, where a number of burn victims from the Pentagon were brought for critical care. A disaster plan was implemented that called for hundreds of patients to be discharged to make way for those more critically injured. Thousands showed up to donate blood, to help in any way possible, and there was one local faith group that wished to "lay hands" on the burn victims for their immediate healing and end to their suffering. While balancing a respect for all religious traditions, a hospital chaplain affirmed the religious belief and intent of the group and offered a distant conference area for the group to pray for those so critically injured in the attack, but also took the opportunity to explain the importance of infection control. The vulnerability of burn victims to infectious agents mandated a sterile environment, a nonnegotiable. Comfort must never be contagious.

For these and future epidemics, we need both science and faith. There are generals who will not go into battle without the presence of chaplains, and there are physicians who understand the treatment of the whole patient, treatment not only of the physical ailment or injury, but also the emotional and spiritual support included in the plan of care. We have a mission and duty to prevent future disasters. We have a commitment to serve one another with comfort care, cultural sensitivity, and respect.

MEASLES

The measles outbreak in upper New York state in an orthodox Jewish community is another example of a public health emergency and a disaster. While measles was wiped out earlier this century, it has come back with a vengeance in certain parts of the country due to a combination of religious belief and refusing immunization.

Measles is highly contagious and a serious respiratory illness and has been the subject of many anti-vaccination advocates that cite religion and cultural reasons for not getting the vaccine. There are almost 1,000 new cases nationally in twenty states as of this writing and children are particularly vulnerable to the disease. Some states have declared public health emergencies. Emotional and spiritual comfort care is needed; however, there are those who feel this disaster could have been avoided if only children and adults had been vaccinated for what is a preventable disease.

In the end, comfort must be sensitive to cultural norms.

NOTE

1. Jerry Griffin, Lancaster, Pennsylvania, chaplain.

Appendix

Comfort: My Pulse Nightclub Deployment Narrative

A deployment narrative is a detailed reflection of how one experienced a disaster. It may include initial notification and a day to day accounting of one's efforts to comfort, as well as an orientation to the unique aspects of the event and an assessment of needs, resources, and tasks. Some narratives are factual, written reports. Others may be stream-of-consciousness impressions that create emotional reactions. Many are a combination of both. These narratives are important communications for supervisors and managers and help "tell the story" of what happened on the disaster deployment. The following is my deployment narrative for the Pulse nightclub mass murder on June 12, 2016, written periodically during my time in Orlando.

Sunday morning, June 12, 2016

Several dead at gay nightclub shooting in Orlando was the news blurb on AOL early this morning out in the cabin. Then the figure jumped to twenty, then forty-nine late in the day. I received my first phone call from Rena in Red Cross staffing early that evening, and even though I had retired five years earlier, after consulting with my husband, I agreed to go and head up the spiritual care team there. Forty-nine dead at a gay nightclub in Florida. I had been to gay nightclubs in Florida.

I called Red Cross travel and booked a flight for early the next morning. I had sent hundreds on deployments when I was national manager at headquarters in Washington, DC. I had supported those on the ground all over the country and had helped write the trainings on what to do and who to do it. But now I was being sent.

Monday, June 13, 2016

Arrived in Orlando and went to the local Red Cross chapter to be oriented. Tried to remember the deployment mantra "flexibility and patience" as I waited to be in-processed. I became a volunteer through the Orlando chapter to expedite obtaining IDs and housing/transportation. I introduced myself to old friends from national headquarters—disaster response really is a family—and determined my first assignment would be the family and friends reception center at the Beardall Senior Citizen Center. It would open Tuesday morning.

I continued to circulate through disaster response headquarters at the chapter, meeting responders, gathering information, and introducing myself to the various activity leads including disaster mental health. Needs were still being assessed and volunteers were continuously arriving throughout the day. Thoughts of past disaster operations continually flooded my mind and I remembered the frustration expressed by other teams that I had deployed: "Hurry up and wait!" Went to the Best Western Airport to get settled in with the rest of the Red Cross team.

Tuesday, January 14, 2016

Arrived early morning at the Beardall Senior Citizen Center and signed in. Management of local volunteers was being handled by the Orlando mayor's office and Orange County leadership. A leadership briefing would be held that morning through local emergency management command and was led by the EMT lead for that shift. Each organization had representation and introduced themselves around the room. Red Cross had a disaster mental health colleague and I attend the briefing.

Yesterday, family members of victims and survivors were sent to the Hampton Inn and later to the Beardall Senior Citizen Center to wait for updates and eventually, for those whose names were not on the list, death notifications. Spontaneous staffing of the Hampton Inn and continuing at the Beardall Center was coordinated by Jim Delgado, a CPE supervisor at Nemours Pediatric Hospital.

All victims and survivors were quickly identified through the assistance of the Federal Emergency Mortuary and death notification provided through Florida law enforcement. The VA Medical Centers deployed their behavioral mental health staff from area and regional hospitals that offered assistance during death notifications and local chaplains and available local clergy and others.

All victims' families and loved ones were notified within thirty-six hours after the event. A number of the victims were from Puerto Rico and Latin America.

Through Saturday evening, the family assistance center (FAC) and all represented agencies providing direct support to the families and impacted community served 482 individuals representing 160 families and 28 persons have returned for continued assistance after returning and reflecting on what other things may be needed.

Disaster spiritual care has been managed at the family assistance center by the Orlando mayor's liaison to the faith community. My task as the disaster spiritual care manager was to support him and empower the local faith community. Building local capacity for future disaster events is also a major goal of our presence. There have been many vigils and remembrance services. There has been an informal memorial developed and expanded in front of the Dr. Philips Performing Arts Center downtown.

The Pulse nightclub is still an active crime scene investigation with no public or family access until the FBI's work is done. Families have requested a site visit, but safety and security are the first priority. This site visit ritual feels very much like an aviation incident. A plane full of gay people hits the ground in one compact area and was flown by a "crazy" Muslim pilot into Disco Mountain. The importance of this ritual cannot be overstated.

When the glitter settles.

There have been many unique requests for emotional and spiritual care. For instance, a request for a blanket might be a way of starting a conversation. The same goes for requests for ribbons and pins from different organizations present. Asking for something is a safe and neutral way to talk to somebody. The faith-based disaster response organizations have gotten much more efficient at mobilizing after horrendous disasters, especially Florida with its own "disaster culture" and greater capacity of trained volunteers.

Under new staffing protocols, spiritual care volunteers can state their availability online and not wait to be recruited or hand-selected. The team in Orlando was partially recruited and partially self-deployed through chapter process. The team is uneven.

Wednesday, June 15, 2016

Since yesterday, disaster spiritual care has staffed the family assistance center and worked side by side with disaster mental health.

This is not a gay disaster. This is a disaster.

Disaster spiritual care and emotional care was provided at the Orlando GLBT Center and outside vigils and memorial services. Federal agencies responding to this disaster sent their GLBT liaisons and GLBT staff to add to the sensitivity of the response. The American Red Cross actively recruited GLBT staff and volunteers to respond to the Pulse nightclub mass shooting. Church of the Brethren disaster childcare was deployed to staff the family assistance center. They have been invaluable. There is much staff support for those staffing the family assistance center.

A needle in a gaystack.

Direct communication has been problematic here in Orlando. Much information has not been captured due to texting and other forms of communication including actually making a telephone call to one another. Instead of asking for something, clients simply Googled for an answer. Same with sharing news.

Thursday, June 16, 2016

At the mayor's press conference this morning, all agencies and organizations were asked to stand behind him during his explanation for what was occurring here, but also to thank those who had responded. I elbowed my way so that I would be standing behind the mayor as a strategy to advocate for appropriate disaster spiritual care. Be visible! I had an opportunity to brief the mayor's chief of staff after the press conference because the behavioral health lead went rogue and did not stay on script and forgot to mention disaster spiritual care needs and resources of these catastrophic disasters, although the Spanish translator did include those in prepared remarks.

Two volunteers were deployed from Puerto Rico, one disaster spiritual care and one disaster mental health. During President Obama and

Vice President Biden's visit on Thursday, both were selected to represent the American Red Cross during the president's private visit with the families of the dead and injured at the Amway Center. It was essential to have language and cultural sensitivity.

Saturday, June 18, 2016

Today, the family assistance center closed early to allow for a previously scheduled professional soccer game. That soccer game also included a tribute to those killed in the disaster and a recognition of those who had responded to support them in the aftermath. There are no more cinnamon rolls in the canteen.

Sunday morning, June 19, 2016

The Pulse nightclub shooting ended almost exactly one week ago.

I'm still on that disaster response high. Last night my colleague, Chaplain Amy, and I attended a Ramadan break the fast service followed by a fundraiser and meal(s) at a mosque in Sanford, Florida. This mosque had been vandalized one week ago after the shooting. It's in the northern Orlando suburbs and many of the members are professionals with extended families. The Islamic Disaster Response of North America has been down here all week working not only with the Islamic faith community but also in developing partnerships with those who have responded to the Orlando mass shooting. The shooter had been identified as a Muslim prompting outrage directed at mosques in the area.

The mosque leadership has already brought in mental health counselors who worked with the children yesterday morning because of threatening fear media and social media exposure.

I had attended another Ramadan service and feast Friday night at the Islamic Center of Orlando and left with the same impression. It was so important to be there, at national level, to express condolences to the Islamic community and not to "blame" them for the attack. Their message to us and to the world was "This is not Islam" and "We, too, strongly condemn the shooting." When the shooter thought about executing the murders, even before he started shooting, he had, in effect, left the faith.

For the Islamic community, there has been accumulated stress and anxiety, not only with fearful children, but also entire family members.

The women's headscarves that proclaim their religion and fear of even leaving the house to do anything.

The family assistance center is anticipated to be open through Wednesday, June 22, with hours from 3–8 p.m.

After these catastrophic events, long-term consequence management emerges particularly in the GLBT community. Increased suicide attempts and successes, domestic violence, unsafe sex, increased rates of HIV infection, and other behavioral issues. At the family assistance center, the GLBT Center is represented with a large presence as well as the GLBT Chamber of Commerce. They have been very busy as families and loved ones come to them for support. In some instances, families not only found out that their loved one was dead but also that they were gay.

One unique aspect of this response has been linking the local chapter in San Juan with the GLBT Center there for partnering for many of the emerging mental health issues family members there will face in the days and months ahead. The GLBT community center there has been marginalized by the government and community and this will give them enhanced visibility and credibility. Logical and vital partnership opportunities in the chapter meeting legitimate needs and with important community initiatives.

Assistance with funerals and travel has been provided by airlines here instantly issuing tickets not only for family members to come to Orlando, but also to take their loved one home. The medical examiner started releasing bodies Wednesday and funerals have been held. Many funerals have also had protesters.

Although a funeral may be held in another country, families have requested spiritual support at funeral homes that have been provided by the local faith community. Again, this is primarily a local response and will need resources for long-term recovery. The One Orlando fund continues to grow and a representative from #BostonStrong has been invited by the mayor to plan for the distribution of donated funds.

Today, I worshipped at the 7:30 a.m. service at St. Mark's AME Church with the mayor's liaison to the faith community. I haven't sung "Kumbya" or "Come by Here" in a long time. It was also Father's Day, which certainly may have an impact on many families impacted by the horrendous disaster. Many theological reflections also include "Prodigal Son" references in religious services. I was welcomed by the pastors and congregation and could sing as loud as I wanted to, or needed to.

There was a moment on the second day when word came down that there were too many chaplains. The mayor's office had purposely over-staffed, as one could not know if there would be a surge on the first day or not knowing what to expect or how to plan for adequate staffing. Spiritual care and mental health were deployed in the FAC and also on the club suites floor above where families were taken for further inter-views with FBI crime investigators. There was also an important faith community piece in this, and, along with the Interfaith Alliance, con-gregations were invited to support those impacted by this event, either here at the Camping World FAC or later with long-term recovery. Over 100 calls were received in the first 6 hours after the letter was emailed. The mayor's office will continue to hold this list and coordinate volun-teers in the days and months ahead.

"I will survive."

One can't help but have one's personal soundtrack for specific life events, and a very soulful and slowed down version of Gloria Gaynor's gay anthem has emerged in my head. Almost all of the best disco songs have great themes for reflection. Donna Summer's "Love Is the Heal-er" I've used before at a memorial service for an AIDS victim when I worked at Cabrini Hospital in New York City.

That soundtrack pops up every now and then because I don't turn on the radio here and have embraced life in a bubble until after the deploy-ment. I did drive through downtown several nights ago and saw all the buildings lit up with rainbow colors and how the world, at least for a few days, claimed to be open, welcoming, and affirming. I know this will not exist for long, but, at least for this week, it is mind-blowing. There's nothing like living in a big, gay world.

Everyone is wearing rainbow this week here, and along with the mass murder last week, to experience the boomerang effect of suddenly being loved bombed is adding to the unreality of today in Orlando.

The janitor sweeping our floor in the staff cafeteria received a call from her son after the shooting to let her know that he was okay, however, she is still sweeping the floor in the cafeteria this week. Many of the victims and survivors came from poorer, minority families, and so very few can take a day off and deal with their own families or themselves and their feelings.

The alligator attack at Disney World took the shooting off the head-lines for a day and one anticipates that attention is already waning for those impacted. A little boy wading at a hotel beach was drowned by an alligator at one of the resorts.

The Sunday newspaper here has a special insert and the front page is full of pictures of the victims. There has been a dedicated effort to say the names of the victims and not just the "number." Say the names.

The Sunday evening community vigil at Lake Eola in downtown Orlando was attended by over 100,000 people and included the clouds opening to reveal a rainbow! The Pulse staff and local gay council-member addressed the group, and the governor was spotted lurking near the band shell but was not welcome to speak. He was spotted leaving the gathering when it became clear that he was not welcome due to his extremely poor record on GLBT issues in the state. This was a vigil for the largest mass shooting in American history [until Las Vegas], not a campaign stop.

Becky, the Red Cross job lead, and I notice that there are few emergency exits or fainting corridors for those who may have a medical emergency or other emergency at the vigil. In disaster, one notices things like that—the basics—bathrooms, exits, and so forth.

Much irony here, the Baptist Church embracing the Unitarian minister, at one of the numerous vigils and memorials here.

We will continue working here through next Wednesday.

Wednesday, June 22, 2019

We concluded our direct services at the family assistance center today. Aside from giving out hundreds of Red Cross blankets and debit cards, there have been hundreds of support moments during our time here—both at Camping World Stadium and various posts in the community. Everything has been available and spontaneous—from survivor support to staff support; I am emotionally and spiritually exhausted.

Tonight is a concert at the Hard Rock Hotel for the survivors and those who traveled to Orlando to support them—the first responders and all the nongovernmental and governmental organizations and agencies—headlined by Imagine Dragons. Red Cross can attend the concert and also staff it, in case there is a breakdown or crises. I put on my patent leather red tennis shoes and notice that I am not alone in my choice of footwear. An instant bond!

My colleague, Chaplain Bonnie, and I encounter a "client" who lost his partner in the shooting and are able to give him a farewell hug.

As a coping strategy, I am drawn on my way out of the concert to a Cinnabon that has just closed. I shamelessly bang on the door still in my Red Cross vest. After a few seconds, I am rewarded with a Cinnabon to take home and eat in my bed at the motel.

Thursday, June 23, 2019

Out processed today and flew home. There has been much stealth mental health support here for staff. I have been given a psychologist for a roommate and have not been ashamed to chat and vent and urge my team to call home often. I try to model self-care but this has been a very hard, personal deployment. They really all are; even with intense clinical training and experience, I couldn't have done this without the support of my husband at home and my disaster spiritual care lead, Tim, in Oregon. It is imperative to take time and report in and manage time so that there is a reflective and renewal part. Those who are exposed to disasters are forever changed by the experience.

Index

About the Author

Earl Johnson was one of the founders of the Spiritual Care function in the American Red Cross. He helped develop the organization's Psychological First Aid curriculum and Coping with Deployment. Johnson worked on "Light Our Way" for the National Voluntary Organizations Active in Disaster.